T0271568

Supporting Positive Behaviour in Intellectual Disabilities and Autism

Supporting Positive Behaviour in Intellectual Disabilities and Autism

Practical Strategies for Addressing Challenging Behaviour

TONY OSGOOD

Jessica Kingsley *Publishers*
London and Philadelphia

First published in 2020
by Jessica Kingsley Publishers
73 Collier Street
London N1 9BE, UK
and
400 Market Street, Suite 400
Philadelphia, PA 19106, USA

www.jkp.com

Library of Congress Cataloging in Publication Data
A CIP catalog record for this book is available from the Library of Congress

British Library Cataloguing in Publication Data
A CIP catalogue record for this book is available from the British Library

ISBN 978 1 78775 132 3
eISBN 978 1 78775 133 0

Printed and bound in Great Britain

This book is for Emma

A small and imperfect gift remains a gift

Acknowledgements

This book was only possible due to my family allowing space and time to write.

Thanks are very much due to Dr Katy Arscot, Krysia Waldock, Maximillian Taken, Helen Coleman, Helen Stone, Tor Townsend and Matthew Gibb for invaluable suggestions and telling silences. Also to Viv Cooper OBE (of the Challenging Behaviour Foundation) for steering ships away from the doldrums.

Contents

CHAPTER 1

Introduction

This little book aims to be accessible, grounded and practical in its advice on challenging behaviour in intellectual or developmental disabilities (IDD), and autistic children and adults. At the same time it raises bigger questions about what challenging behaviour means, how we think of it and the ways we respond.

The book is written with support workers, parents and family carers, advocates, managers and personal assistants in mind, though it will benefit professionals, also. This book does not replace the need for informed and accountable advice to be sought, but it does suggest approaches that often help and ways of thinking that make complex situations clear. The advice contained in this book is based upon best practice guidance concerning what is currently termed positive behaviour support (PBS). As such, the style of the book blends informal and interesting sources with more formal ones.

To inform how we respond to challenging behaviour it is best to know why it happens. If we are not clear on the *why*, the *how* can go awry. To begin to explore *why*, three questions can be asked:

- Is the person well, living an interesting and meaningful life, surrounded by people they like and who like them enough to support them well?

- Is the person's ability to communicate recognised and responded to?

- What events regularly predict and follow the challenging behaviour?

In the thirty years I have worked to support people to understand challenging behaviour there have been three major changes to how we think about such behaviours:

- We now understand that challenging behaviour is meaningful for the person. Before thinking about how to support someone, we need to understand what the behaviour achieves for the individual.

- We now understand that behaviour can be thought of as communication. This helps us to see that teaching new ways of behaving and communicating is essential. A plan lacking strategies to aid communication is a poor plan.

- We now know quality of life is an intervention in and of itself, not a future goal. A life without rapport, friendship, opportunities to make choices and learn, a life lacking activities to enjoy, is a poor life.

Waiting for challenging behaviour to disappear before increasing choice and opportunities means the person may never qualify for an ordinary life. They will live a life caught in a limbo between their severe reputation and a desirable future. Such waiting exacerbates challenging behaviour. Worse still, people using services may simply give up.

The above three 'innovations' seem common sense today, hindsight being what it is. The principles – a functional approach, a communication focus, a quality of life agenda – underpin this book, and align with current advice on best practice, which seems to be incorporated within the term *positive behaviour support*. We are fortunate to have at our disposal a great deal of knowledge concerning challenging behaviour. The people who paid the highest price in gathering such knowledge were often not professionals or researchers: the lives of children and adults with IDD or autistic adults and children and their families are littered with tales of broken promises and hurt as often as glowing tales of achievement. They have learned the hard way.

There is a growing expectation for families (and those who know the person well) to be an inherent part of searching for an understanding of challenging behaviour, as well as being a central pillar of our attempts to craft solutions. It is not always the case that the views of families are taken seriously, and the knowledge of direct support staff is often ignored: the voices of professionals tend to dominate conversations, their views tend to dominate narratives about challenging behaviour, they speak over the experiences of others. This book suggests that effective behavioural support features 'dispersed leadership', meaning no individual voice dominates. Dispersed leadership includes people in decisions regardless of qualifications or status.

Leadership is not about those with specialist knowledge telling others what to do. Leadership involves a good deal of listening to those who do the actual work or those who experience support. No one is voiceless even if they do not speak. A good leader knows behaviour is communication and so they listen with their eyes as well as their ears. They know being 'voiceless' does not trap people; they know Serviceland is often poor at listening. The poor treatment too many people using Serviceland receive is not due to a lack of voice, but a lack of power.

A good leader makes a safe space for people to share their perspectives, and a good leader shares power and decision-making. Effective leadership guides rather than tells and it enables people who know how to get on with things to go get on with them. A good leader is usually a practice leader – someone who leads by example, demonstrates what works, explains why, and so teaches through doing.

It is not leadership to pop in on someone's life for twenty minutes, make a few suggestions in a letter or report, and then take no responsibility for when things go wrong, or take credit for when things go right. It is still too common for busy professionals to pass briefly through people's lives without meeting the person they encounter.

Several years ago Dave Hingsburger – a Canadian activist and teacher – asked a class of professionals how many children or adults with disabilities they knew through working with them. We all plucked a figure from the air. He asked us again. How many did we *know*? I am not the brightest of people but even I suspected there was more to his question than met the ear. So I *actively* listened as Dave asked us the same question for the third time.[1] The number of people with disabilities that I had come to *know* as opposed to merely *worked with* was shamefully small. It's the difference between encountering a person or *meeting* them.

We encounter many people but we *know* only a few: to know someone is to be shared with – their preferences, their views, the thinking and feeling aspects of themselves.

To meet someone *other* than ourselves is an act of profound bravery. When you meet a person you discover what is important to them but you need to be worthy and useful to the people you encounter in order for them to trust you enough so they share. Only then do you *meet* others, only then do you begin to *know* others. That knowing is a privilege available only to those who invest time in taking the person seriously (for more information, see Hingsburger, 1996, 1998).

This book encourages readers to *meet* those labelled with IDD or autistic people for real. It teaches us about the importance of remaining authentic and genuine in our attempts to get to *know* people. *Their* stories are not about us. Even if our training and status makes us someone considered an authority, we are a minor character in a story concerning them.

To not listen to people wealthy in knowledge about what is helpful in supporting a person is akin to visiting a foreign nation without an understanding of the language, culture or customs: we place ourselves at immediate disadvantage. To find our way about it benefits us to find local guides. A good leader listens hard to local knowledge. A good leader doesn't feel obliged to be in charge.

---

1   Active listening means taking not only what is said at face value – a literal interpretation – but also what is meant. To listen actively we decode words or behaviour into meaning. A person may say or appear upset, but why? It incorporates careful listening and watching, but only in preparation of taking action to support the person in a manner that shows we are very much present with them. An autistic young man I spent time with would frown after a time together. The frown meant to me that I was speaking too fast, too unclearly. His behaviour showed me I needed to slow down, give him space and time to think.

Something Like A Soapbox

When I first started working alongside people with IDD and autistic people whose behaviour was considered challenging, I was impressed with how much I knew, and I hoped others would be equally impressed. In hindsight, it is amazing how little insight I had about how little I knew. That did not stop me communicating (or at least broadcasting) a great deal about how little I knew to practically anyone who would listen, or who at least were not fast enough to escape.

In those days there was an emphasis on simply stopping what we then called problem behaviour.[2] We placed the problem of behaviour in the person ('she *has* problem behaviour'), though where she kept it heaven only knew. In time we began to speak instead of *challenging behaviour*, implying the issue was often for those *around* the person. Those supporting others were rarely taught about the benefits of communication or working to grow rapport or to support someone to get the life they wished for or needed. We did not understand challenging behaviour was both a complaint and a symptom, even though many parents and support staff knew this fundamental truth. They had learned lessons from their experiences and their loving a child or adult whose behaviour was often confounding to us, clear to them.

Without such insights, people made use of abusive and punishing techniques. In part this was due to people with IDD or autistic people not being considered full partners: how they felt did not seem to matter, what they *did* was the only thing we counted. The things that they did were seen as products of their differences, their pathologies. Such differences were considered as making them less worthy of being listened to or taken seriously. In this way many professionals reflected the general zeitgeist: society preferred to not see disability because society was not about diversity but about fitting in. God help you if you did not fit, because society wouldn't. Those institutions set up to care for those people at the edges of society (the churches, the hospitals, the children's homes) were often most ardent in their use of pain and punishment; but even in purgatory, voices were raised that questioned what was done in the name of science or moral correction.

---

2   We considered it a problem to be overcome or eliminated rather than understood; challenging behaviour couldn't teach anything to those of us who seemed to know so much.

At the heart of society's terrible error was a simple truth, laid bare in report after report concerning hospital scandals: we often did things *to* people, not *with* them. People who needed support received it in exchange for their dignity; they paid for intervention by surrendering little bits of their humanity.

We didn't notice because we didn't need to heed their voices. We were too busy measuring the things we considered important to actually notice the voids in their lives. We did not record the families and places they mourned. We did record behaviour, bowel movements and medication. We did not think to measure loneliness or heartache.

When a person labelled with IDD or an autistic person was admitted to a long-stay hospital or other service they often were obliged to leave behind their family, their identity and their friendships at the door. We had new identities pre-designed and waiting; we had new words and new expectations. They wore the new clothes provided for them by the powerful and were expected to behave as patients, not people. Even the words they began to use to define themselves were borrowed from the language of the people in charge. For example, people would refer to themselves as 'high grades' in line with the supposed 'level of ability' determined by assessment. People became less human, more a number. This dehumanising appeared to give greater power to professionals to do as they wished. For too many people using services, dignity and respect were things that happened to other people.

An institution is a place but also a way of thinking. An institution boxes and processes people, it seeks to strip people of their identities in exchange for prescriptive definitions about who and what they are. An institution can house many hundreds of people but sometimes only two or three. We foolishly believed closing large institutions and moving people (often without their consent) on to smaller community services would solve the problem of institutionalisation. But we have cleverly managed to replicate how large institutions worked in these smaller community-based homes – customs and practices continue though the net curtains are cleaner. Too often smaller bastions of institutionalising thinking and practice have been created, and lionised as examples of good practice. Institutions are alive and well because the thinking that produces them remains rife.

Practically all hospital scandal inquiries that have shone a light into abusive practices in the UK have concluded the same sordid lessons over the last fifty years:

- Dehumanising practices are nurtured not by bad apples but by bad systems that allow the rot to be normalised and go unquestioned.

- An institution is run for the benefit of people working there, not living there.

- People living in institutions might as well be things.

In this regard it matters not the size of the building: being unheard in a large institution is the same as being unheard in a small community home, save for the lack of secret places harbouring safety and privacy. There is no place to hide in a small home.[3]

Whilst we have moved on a good deal and the acceptability of controlling responses to challenging behaviour is lessening, this is by no means a battle won. Travesties such as punishing consequences to challenging behaviour, the horror of children and adults being placed miles from their families in institutions, and utterly avoidable deaths are still regularly reported.

In 2011, in the UK, the BBC documentary series *Panorama* revealed the abuse of autistic people and people with IDD resident in a private hospital called Winterbourne View. The hospital was part of an organisation providing care for vulnerable people while making a profit for shareholders. Following a criminal investigation, prosecutions were made. As a result, those controlling policy sought to move people whose behaviour was most challenging away from such large congregate settings as hospitals and assessment units, to smaller and more local services. The government initiative *Transforming Care* promised to ensure most people being supported in hospitals were found better support elsewhere, and the NHS, which often funded such private hospital placements, proclaimed a need for homes not hospitals. But promises are easier to say than deliver. After half a

---

3   For a useful, nuanced and salutary ethnography of what it is like to work in a community home that is almost like an institution, see Levinson, 2010. Some things, it turns out, are hard to change.

dozen years of investing in endless assessing and subsidising rhetoric, some people's lives have been enriched through escaping hospital, but for too many autistic people and those with IDD not much has changed. The *Transforming Care* initiative appears to be no more than continuing indifference: people remain miles from home and their voices continue to be unheard.

This Book

This book will not change your life, but aims to provoke thinking. That thinking might change how you understand challenging behaviour – and that can change lives for the better.

Had I written this book thirty years ago it would have been very different. It would have emphasised behaviour analytic approaches and de-emphasised relationships and quality of life. It would have been more about data than people's stories and more about the technology of behavioural science than about choice.

Now we know the benefits of listening to the voices and behaviour of the children and adults we serve, there is no longer any excuse for blocking our ears. When I work with people whose behaviour challenges, I have learned, primarily, to turn up, shut up and listen. Like many, I've learned to listen with my eyes. Most of the people I know are better non-verbal communicators than verbal. To listen watchfully sounds a little odd, but it cuts to the heart of the work.

The old default of harvesting data before anything else has been amended by experiences accruing from the benefits of listening to people's stories of their lives. Now I ask about relationships and well-being before antecedents and contingency data. Now I ask what's bugging them, not about schedules of reinforcement.

When at times this book questions and criticises common or robotic practices, remember that I myself have engaged in unhelpful and actively bad habits at times.[4] Invariably such moments coincided with the demands of my job but that's no defence. Putting my own interests first may be logical in some situations, but it means other

---

4   I'm not proud of this, but reflecting upon my errors has helped me become a more person-centred practitioner. Being reflective and person centred means I always have a handy pin to make use of in order to pop any inflated opinion of myself.

people come second. John O'Brien – of whom, much more later – writes that a person-centred practitioner lives and works in the tensions between the individual they are supporting and the incessant demands of organisations to deliver quantity not quality. Being person centred means we are caught between the sea of faces and the kingdom of numbers that is Serviceland (O'Brien, 2002).

I am in recovery from the kingdom of numbers, however, being in a kind of rehab for behaviourists. Each day provides opportunities for me to be better at being more rounded and more person centred not only in my work, but in my whole life.

This book shows that if *we* know where challenging behaviour comes from we may feel more able to confront people who say it comes out of nowhere. There is always a predictor that challenging behaviour is likely to appear, usually obvious warning signs, too. Whether we see these or not is the issue.

If we know *why* challenging behaviour keeps happening, we might be better placed to do something constructive about it. If we know *when* challenging behaviour is likely, we can work to amend those moments. If we know what *follows* challenging behaviour, we can find easier ways for the person to achieve the same outcome in a safer manner. These approaches may well enable the person not to challenge quite so often or so intensely.

There are always alternatives we can support the person (and ourselves) to learn. We cannot guarantee to stop challenging behaviour – humans don't unlearn – but we can make it the least effective skill the person has learned. We can help make challenging behaviour obsolete, or less impactful, or less significant by supporting the person to find new ways of achieving their very reasonable desires as part of a life they enjoy. This book is an informal (and occasionally funny and often sad) guide to doing just this.

Who Shaped the Thoughts that Made this Book?

We all have heroes – people who have given us pause for thought and so shaped our thinking. The best ideas in this book are crafted from the work of others, though the errors I claim for myself. The

American psychologist Herb Lovett once gave a speech long ago – in the ancient 1990s – that suggested Serviceland had difficulty in learning: though they tend to be filled with learned people, human service organisations often do not learn from the feedback provided by people using services. People that challenge may be difficult to serve but it does not follow we are obliged to degrade them by not giving authority to their experiences, pain and gifts.

Lovett widened the debate about how best to support those whose behaviour challenges us. He spoke of community as not merely a place but a way of being connected with people. Community is not a place, he argued, but a way of life. Lovett dared to speak of the need for a more compassionate application of scientific knowledge. And he dared to speak of love.

Lovett was an activist who questioned how behavioural approaches were being used. He suggested it is all too easy to be blind to the person or their lives when seeking to reduce challenging behaviour. He argued the use of aversive and punishing techniques, an over-reliance on restraints and medication, and intervening without knowing about the person, are self-defeating and inhuman. He argued we have created services for what people are not, not who they are. Basing intervention on a diagnosis and not a person is similarly unhelpful. The price of such situations is paid not by managers or commissioners or services but through the denuded experiences of many people trying to live their lives in or through services. Lovett's point is that by focusing purely on behaviour it is all too easy to miss the big things that are important to a person, such as living a good life. By focusing on data we blind ourselves to the equally important human perspective.

A graph does not describe a person, and scatter plots are merely ink on paper. These things inform our practice. We reduce a person to a diagnosis or a problem and lose sight of the human if we fail to consider broader quality-of-life issues. Supporting people whose behaviour challenges the system was for Lovett not a clinical issue, more a social justice issue (Lovett, 1996).

There is plenty of research to show that having few friends or limited social networks can be debilitating (e.g., Forrester-Jones *et al.*, 2006). Likewise, not keeping life interesting and active, not being person centred, is a road we really do not want to travel if we are committed to good support (Mansell and Beadle-Brown, 2012). But no matter the quality of the organisation, if support provision does not continually renew the support it provides it will deteriorate to resemble something like an institution: a factory churning out clinical misery. Someone using services might value choice and voice – and the unpredictability (the freedom) this might produce – as much as how their support staff are efficiently organised. If human services paid as much attention to the accomplishment of an enjoyable life as they do to other issues, many people would be better supported, including staff and parents (European Intellectual Disability Research Network, 2003).

David Pitonyak works to help people support more effectively those who challenge; he argues loneliness is the only real disability as it sets us apart. Pitonyak wonders if by reaching for 'independent living' we are not at times inadvertently creating islands of loneliness (Pitonyak, 2010b). His work, emphasising belonging and partnership alongside robust evidenced-based interventions, continues to inspire and will feature throughout this small book. Pitonyak argues that a crucial and often overlooked aspect of how we respond to challenging behaviour involves acting to ensure we consider the welfare of those supporting people, too: do support workers and parents or siblings have their own support plans, Pitonyak wonders, and if not, why not?

Dependence on support services means many disabled people rely on others. Relying on others makes it immensely important that services are competent at delivering what the person requires. The question of competence is a complex one from the outset; the first problem is who defines competent provision: the accountants, the commissioners or the people living in services? If it is the former two, then managerialism wins and the human can become lost in a field of financial figures and bottom lines. Human lives cannot be run as businesses. Pitonyak, along with many others, argues for both good 'clinical' skills and inclusion of the views of people living in services.

Humans tend to be safer and have richer experiences the greater the number of people with widely different views they have in their lives. Often most of the people involved in the life of a person with IDD or autistic individuals are paid to be there. In the UK, many people with impactful differences are living lives in a market economy that views them not as customers but as economic units and assets. John O'Brien wrote powerfully that discovering the person within the myths is crucial, and that what matters is the accomplishment of a good quality of life (O'Brien, 1987). Influenced by the work of John and his wife Connie Lyle O'Brien, this book is aimed in part at helping us remember that those who challenge us are fully human first, that those challenges are no excuse not to do our best with and by people, and that people are not merely resources to help grow a pension fund for chief executive officers.

'What Happened to Learning Disability? What is Autism?'

This book is about challenging behaviour, but given that behaviour does not occur unless there is someone to behave, and given that one cannot understand behaviour unless one understands the person and their contexts, *and* given that autism and intellectual disabilities are significant influences on people, let us define some terms.

Anyone encountering the term *learning disabilities* might be forgiven for thinking this group of people are unable to learn. This is not the case. People with *learning disabilities* are quite able to learn if given skilled teaching, though it might take more time and more opportunities. Learning *difficulties* – from an international perspective – is applied to those with specific learning issues such as dyslexia. So to help international understanding, the UK is adopting the term IDD. This is the term I will use.

Whilst I remain uneasy with the word *disability,* personally much preferring *difference,* IDD is understood internationally, and it shows more precisely what we are talking about: an impactful difference in skills or learning present prior to adulthood, often requiring ongoing support. Intellectual disability means a measurable intelligence (IQ) below 70 (though IQ is a contested concept and is difficult to measure with certainty), and the need for support in some areas of life. To help organise support, different 'severities' of IDD are identified. Those with mild IDD often enjoy a good quality of independent life with minimal support. The more profoundly a person is impacted by IDD, the greater their reliance on the abilities and sensibilities of others.

Genetic or biological issues often cause IDD, but social factors are also important: this is true with regard to challenging behaviour, also. We can attribute a child's behaviour to their condition and easily ignore the fact they are simply unhappy or have toothache. This diagnostic overshadowing means we only see the most obvious issue, missing the elephant in the room. We need to ensure we do not think of the person through the dimensions of their diagnosis. It's most helpful to think of *any* IDD as not determining what people can or cannot achieve.

Disability, however we think of it, not only shapes our thinking and behaviour, but it also shapes what we do and how we respond to people so labelled. Knowing about possible or probable 'characteristics' can help our understanding, providing it does not blind us to the uniqueness of the individual. There are some things I am fairly good at (like cooking, like swimming, like avoiding writing this book for ten years) and other things I am utterly terrible at[5] (staying calm about things that matter to me, dancing the tarantella to Tom Waits, not asking questions, eating less – this list is *endless*). So you might say I have what we call a 'spiky profile of skills'. I cannot dance too well but I can waddle with gusto. But there are *always* alternatives to dancing. We humans are as mottled in our varying abilities as a forest floor in autumn. We are each a complex mosaic of abilities. And those abilities are enabled by where we live and whom we're with. This does not mean those of us with specific issues do not require specific skilled support. It simply means cut-out solutions will not be as beneficial as individualised solutions. Cut-out solutions have their appeal to those organising things, but the end result is often compromise. The *average* legroom in a car or airline does not suit my *particular* height, let me attest.

In terms of autism, I adhere to current convention, namely the identity-first use of 'autistic', hence my writing of an autistic child or adult. I shall be writing more about autism as the book continues, but autism threads its way through the whole. Autism means different

---

5   Though it begs the question, who judges and to whose standards?

things to different people but most accept it is a difference in neurology that results in autistic people usually experiencing the world in a way unfamiliar to neurotypicals – that is, non-autistic people. Autism is not lesser, autism is not disorder, autism is difference. Autistic people often experience the world as it is whereas non-autistic people see the world they wish to.

What is Challenging Behaviour?

Challenging behaviour is any behaviour that puts at risk well-being, health and cultural norms, and that has an impact on relationships or status. It can annoy you somewhat, or endanger life. Challenging behaviours are impactful. Challenging behaviour is a summary label for a myriad of behaviours that hurt or harm. We might find some or all of the behaviours below challenging, depending on *where* the person is, *who* the person is, how *often* they happen, how *intensely* they occur, and our ability to understand *why* it happens:

- swearing

- screaming

- hitting others

- kicking others

- pulling hair

- hurting themselves

- eating or consuming harmful things

- running away

- withdrawing from activities

- ignoring someone.

It is often the case that the person behaving in these ways may not intend to cause harm, may not even think of their behaviour as challenging at all. They may consider it self-determination, self-preservation, or self-expression. They may not consider it at all. Challenging behaviour then is both very real *and* a 'social construction', in that behaviour is said to be challenging when people agree it is. A young man's smoking and drinking is not a problem for him or his friends, but it might well be considered challenging by teetotal non-smoking neighbours or the class teacher, and his doctor might want to tell him about future risks, too. The young man might well consider everybody's advice to him unbearably challenging and harmful to his sense of independent identity.

Just because behaviour is socially unacceptable in one place (removing clothing in the frozen-food aisle of a supermarket) does not mean it is unacceptable in another place (getting ready for bed). The impact on cultural norms influences whether others classify behaviour as challenging. But here is the issue: who decides? And what happens when you are so labelled? Can you appeal such a decision?

Even when a person who does not know you classifies your behaviour as challenging, that behaviour remains meaningful for you. No matter how unusual or impactful, the behaviour is adaptive – it has an effect and is fit for the situation you find yourself in. It will continue to be used until other behaviours are learned. And even if alternative behaviour is learned, the person may choose the behaviour that is most effective – often, the most impactful.

This can result in the meaning of challenging behaviour becoming contested and politicised: a young person harming themselves may be diagnosed with a 'psychiatric disorder' by a psychiatrist, a 'behavioural disorder' by a psychologist, or as possessing a 'coping mechanism' by others. Challenging behaviour is often all things to all people, though the most powerful people tend to write the historic notes that follow the person throughout their lives. Such diagnoses litter the histories of a vulnerable child or adult in the same way plastic litters the ocean: both cause harm, both drag you down, both can become part of you, and both can kill.

The Challenging Behaviour Foundation (CBF) is the leading UK charity supporting families of those with IDD whose behaviour challenges those around them. The CBF estimates that in the UK alone up to 30,000 individuals with severe IDD show challenging behaviour. Challenging behaviour is a significant feature of the lives of many more children with moderate or mild IDD. It has a significant cost in terms of resources, time, exhaustion and happiness. Challenging behaviour is a significant element of parental concern and the work of professionals the world over. Wherever we go, there it is.

What Causes Challenging Behaviour?

There are a great number of factors that might contribute to challenging behaviour, some of which are more important than others, depending on the individual. We know there is incredibly strong evidence that much challenging behaviour is learned and maintained by simple reinforcement. Much of this book addresses these ecological factors. The reason we often look at the ecology – the places and people around the individual – to account for challenging behaviour, is because the fit between the person and those around them is often vital in working out why challenging behaviour happens. If there are conflicts, we are likely to see challenging behaviour.

Environmental factors that should be considered and amended include:

- access to activities, food and people the individual prefers

- being involved in decisions and having choice

- having a life with structure and predictability without routines becoming institutionalised (we need routines not regimes)

- the communication abilities and opportunities available

- the noise levels, type of lights, how busy and unpredictable a place is

- having people who have realistic expectations and know the person well: evidence of trust and good rapport.

There are also factors that are internal to the person. Medical issues, such as illnesses or pain, can make us less tolerant of things we might otherwise be able to cope with (my family know I have a PhD in Grumpy when suffering near-terminal Man Flu). Ascertaining if the person is in pain may be problematic because sometimes the person cannot tell us directly, but we can pick up clues from changes in behaviour. A full medical examination is usually helpful to eliminate such possibilities: a person may not be pathologically pre-disposed to self-harm but might have toothache. Some forms of genetic or physiological conditions can impact behaviour. Therefore, health checks and monitoring of well-being are the first step to understanding what influences challenging behaviour.

Other personal factors include emotional or mental health. How we feel and think matters a good deal, and influences how we act. Our sense of self, our sense of belonging in a place or among a network of equal relationships, our ability to communicate, and our needs and desires, all combine to influence our behaviour. That is why throughout this book I urge us to keep a look-out for elephants in the room before calling on behavioural assessments.

If you can ensure good communication, an interesting life and basic physiological and psychological well-being, you tend to find you have facilitated a reduction in challenging behaviours without the need for other support.

This has led me to conclude that all too often challenging behaviour is complaining about something not working in the person's life. We should arrange what the person needs for a happy life rather than reprimand them for challenging behaviour: challenging behaviour may be the only language they have that is sure to make you hear.

Why Does Challenging Behaviour Persist?

Any behaviour that works in getting or avoiding things will continue. If you are working with someone whose behaviour challenges then that behaviour is being maintained (you will have heard the term *reinforced* at some point: this is what it means). A child outgrows her 'terrible twos' because she learns new things when her parents learn new ways of teaching and being with her. *She* does not so much grow up, we grow *her*. The screaming reduces when talking begins, but *only* if her parents enable her talking. If the child's needs are not met by being shown more effective ways of achieving them, the screaming persists.

I know you and I were both saint-like teenagers and above reproach, but those others were just terrible, weren't they? The reason they stopped behaving so terribly is because they learned alternative ways of thinking and doing ('Learning is growing up,' one young person confided to me). But until we learn new ways of doing things we will continue doing what works – be it screaming, hitting or a tantrum – but the good news is we can teach and learn new tricks.

When someone we know ignores our words, when we are unheard and unloved, when our pain goes unnoticed, we *will* be more likely to demonstrate those tantrum behaviours we acquired at the age of two. Having a wide repertoire of behaviours to call on can come in handy in a tight fix. Having a range of behaviours available for common situations is the Swiss Army Knife for humans.

Many children and adults with IDD have struggled to learn new ways of doing things and many people supporting them have struggled to learn how to teach. Old habits die hard, especially when they work, especially when there are few alternatives. For example, if I have learned people will not listen when I ask but will listen when I scream, my screaming is reinforced by people listening, and screaming will remain useful for me. So is behaviour a failure of an ability to learn, or a failure of our ability to teach?

We need to remember we all once had to learn everything we have forgotten we know: to express ourselves, to ask, to drive, to write, to sing about referees not divine mediators, to read quirky books about challenging behaviour. Expecting a child to know intrinsically how to behave in a certain way is not going to help that child's learning. We create and craft our children every day. And what we teach our children, they show as adults. Challenging behaviour can last a long time when few alternatives exist. Challenging behaviour can last a long time when it is reinforced.

'Just Reprimand People Who Challenge; That Worked for Me!'

Did it though? We all benefit from boundaries and knowing right from wrong, helpful from unhelpful behaviour, but life is more complex than we sometimes admit. There are times when the rules of appropriateness are determined by who we are rather than what we do. Telling people off for their behaviour when it is the only behaviour they know is like criticising a New Zealand five-year-old for not speaking a Kashubian dialect unknown outside a village in northern Poland: obscure and unhelpful.

Besides, punishment is counter-productive, even if we ignore the ethics of someone big or powerful harming someone small and powerless. If a child is often fearful of being criticised or corrected, what happens to that child's sense of self? Humans have this funny knack of learning even when there is no formal teaching going on, and early accidental experiences can stay with us for a lifetime. Some of us might learn to welcome being punished – because any form of attention is attention, even if it is intended to be a telling-off – and do we really want to create a human who enjoys punishment? That is a gift that will keep on giving through the generations.

We can easily skew young humans by withholding praise, clear communication and boundaries, and we can scar them by drowning them in unthinking condemnation, fake praise and real hurt. I have worked with too many people whose only form of a hug is known, colloquially, as physical restraint, and too many people who enjoy hurting the feelings of others.

Too many lives have been twisted into cruel shapes by punishment. I humbly believe there has been a mis-translation of behavioural science when applied to the real world and suggest that if we use the rod we will spoil the child.

We want to suffer the child, not make the child suffer. One thing *is* worth considering though: we cannot blame our own authoritarian tendencies on God (Blaug, 2000).

What Is Positive Behaviour Support?

Positive behaviour support (PBS) is an umbrella term that describes approaches to constructively understand and respond to challenging behaviour. By constructive, we mean approaches that focus on growing new ways of behaving without resorting to using aversive or punishing techniques. PBS will be referred to throughout this book.

PBS grew out of dissatisfaction at what was custom and practice: an over-reliance on aversive ways of dealing with challenging behaviour. Aversive approaches often dehumanised people, and included:

- physically restraining people

- hurting people

- using medication to dull people

- threatening or scaring people

- keeping people isolated

- taking away things that matter to the person

- managing behaviour rather than supporting people.

Many interventions focused on doing things *following* an incident – a little like designing a shoddy stable door long after the horse has bolted. It was very common for people whose behaviour challenged to be placed in 'time-out' – places or spaces where they were not given attention, or were isolated from the things they liked or needed. PBS demands people ask more about time-in than time-out. PBS asks us to consider how we can build skills rather than punish people.

When people ask me what PBS is, I suggest it is about catching people being good or doing well, and reinforcing what is helpful, rather than punishing what is not. If we paid more attention to people when they are not challenging, a lot of upset could be avoided. Even more can be avoided if we teach people they simply do not need to challenge to get what they need or avoid what they do not.

And if only we created spaces that were designed around people, rather than fitting them in to what we have pre-assembled, life would be far easier and probably far less expensive.

There are many definitions of PBS, but most include the following:

- an improvement in lifestyle (supporting the person to live a life they prefer)

- use of functional assessment to identify why behaviour is happening

- use of many interventions that, like a mosaic, when seen together, make a picture of coherent support

- making the place the person lives fit for them (we call these *ecological changes*)

- setting things up to avoid conflicts (we call these *antecedent interventions*)

- teaching *new skills* to people using and providing support

- enriching a person's life with lots of activities, people and things the person enjoys

- not using aversive or punishing strategies

- a long-term perspective: PBS wants to fix the future by fixing today

- the voices of people using support are as important as others

- PBS makes use of various approaches to help support people, for example person-centred planning, psychological, nursing and other perspectives (MacDonald and McGill, 2013).

PBS grew from the blending of values-led approaches and applied behaviour analysis (ABA). This blending of science and person-centred approaches is at times uneasy (Kincaid, 2017), but including wider perspectives has enriched ABA. For families and people using services, PBS simply seeks to deliver what the person needs for a good life in a non-humiliating and non-harming manner (Carr *et al.*, 1999).

An assessment service that excludes person-centred approaches or does not include communication or life-enhancement, an environment that uses punishment, that does not feature partnership working with family and friends, that restricts access to the people, places and things a person *needs,* is not a place using PBS, no matter what it claims. It is more likely to be an inefficient old-fashioned and discredited place.

Sometimes there are easy clues to the charade: if a place refers to itself as 'a unit', you can be pretty sure the minds that designed it have simply added a façade of 'PBS' over the top of their disquieting archaeology and institutional working. They have simply rebadged old thinking and practices.

No doubt you have heard of 'fool's gold': let me assure you there is also 'fool's PBS'. It glitters and appears to sparkle but the shine soon rubs off for the people living there. It is easy to *claim* PBS, but truly hard work to do it well.

What Is Quality of Life?

Quality of life is a subjective experience. What makes my life enjoyable and worthwhile is likely different from what enriches yours. There are a good many serviceable definitions of quality of life, but I think of it as people enjoying interesting active lives within equitable relationships in places they like.

Too often people with IDD do not experience the opportunities to live the same good quality of life afforded to their non-disabled peers. They encounter barriers from systems intended to support them: they experience attitudes that limit them, and they face poverty, discrimination and powerlessness. Those with IDD whose behaviour challenges others are frequently particularly short-changed when it comes to the things that often make a life worth living.

We often see quality of life referred to as 'QoL'. Acronyms are useful in journals and books but not in real life: acronyms have the ring of jargon and are a shortcut in thinking. In real life, when speaking about it or contributing to it, it is best to spell out 'quality of life' in its full, explicit and colourful detail. The same is true when working to improve it: there are no shortcuts. Do not skimp on quality of life: it is the job of services to deliver it. Acronyms and shorthand will simply short-change quality of life, and not do it justice.

John O'Brien suggests that we would do well to consider five important principles when gauging whether someone has a good quality of life (O'Brien, 1987). These questions are as relevant today as ever, but we are perhaps as far away from making the delivery of a quality of life our central mission as ever.

- Can we demonstrate that our work is respectful to the choices of the person? (If the person cannot clearly tell us, can we interpret their actions as communicating whether what we hope we do is what they prefer?)

- Does our work to support the person actively connect them with the local community?

- Does our work to support the person ensure they are not at the periphery of community or otherwise set apart, but part of the community?

- A person who is increasing their skills is a person growing future options, and O'Brien asks us to ensure we organise ways to help the individual grow their competence.

- Do we, O'Brien wonders, respect the dignity of the person, not only in small matters, but also in things that are more significant to the person?

Onwards

This book draws together thirty years of experience and current research in an informal, entertaining and informed manner. It presents situations that are sad and funny and demonstrate the hard work required to support those whose behaviour challenges. We will go searching for invisible elephants before encountering battling robots and humans. Along the way we will stand upon soapboxes, rage against inequality, make mention of compassion, and explore simple ways to interpret the messages behind challenging behaviour. All before suggesting clear ways for developing support strategies without the need to roll around the floor in despair. *All* without use of a safety net.

CHAPTER 2

Manifesto

A Bill of Rights (and Wrongs)

People with agendas and biases have written every book you have ever read. Some writers are more explicit about their biases than others, and so it seems best to acknowledge my own.

1. *It is your right to have people with expertise support decisions that help you.* Those with the most expertise about you are you, your family or friends, the people who know you best, the people you trust. Professionals must work in partnership with such experts in order to develop an understanding of what you need and want. It is wrong to think others have a quick solution. Avoid the discourse that says hospitals or assessment units are the solution to all woes: they are not. Locking people away is not a solution. Too often such places are the insidious problem whispering for us to abdicate our abilities to cope. It is utterly feasible to provide a great quality of life and good support for those with impactful challenging behaviour in ordinary homes and schools. It takes hard work and imagination: we need to be better at organising commitment to provide what research has shown is more than possible. It can be done because it is being done all over the world. Do not let others steal your agency or undermine your belief in your ability to work with what is in front of you.

2. *It is right to face up to the real difficulties you face, though unhelpful to focus solely on challenging behaviour.* We should forgive ourselves because we *all* tend to respond to anything

that is surprising, bizarre or just plain disgusting. Rather than fix behaviour, fix the life, then often the behaviour becomes less of an issue. Reframe the focus away from the behaviour. Rather than gathering information *only* for challenging behaviour, gather it for the good things that happen, or near misses – when we avoid challenging behaviour. Work out why good things happen and learn to do those things more often. Keep a balanced view. The reality is a person's challenging behaviour is likely to consume a small percentage of their time. The final important element of this principle is that we never fix the behaviour to tolerate a broken environment. What value is our work if it does not contribute to the person's quality of life?

3. *It is right to wonder what challenging behaviour is telling us.* We can do this by conducting a person-centred functional assessment, or we can use other methods to listen to what is possibly meant by the behaviour. Challenging behaviour is often a complaint that despite our best efforts we are not quite doing what the person needs. It is hard to hear such complaints, especially at 3am when we are tired, but if challenging behaviour is happening, it is being reinforced and has meaning for the person. Let us listen better and work out what the clues are telling us, and more importantly, unflinchingly respond positively in ways that do not eliminate the future.

4. *It is right to base support on your preferences and needs.* It is wrong to receive support that is not person centred and designed to meet the unique preferences, gifts and needs of the person. Fit support around the person, do not parachute the person into existing ideas or places. Take a human view of humans in distress. Behavioural science helps our work but it is not the whole of our work.

5. *It is right to use rights.* Sometimes it takes the work of many to enable the rights of one person or a family. Rights need to be pursued. People whose behaviour is considered challenging have the same human rights as everybody else: they are full members of our diverse and vibrant society. Families of children whose behaviour challenges are first and foremost

families. Families have rights and should expect advice tailored to their own culture and requirements. It is wrong not to challenge things that are unhelpful, and we need to stop pretending every service or parent or professional is good. Nobody is perfect and everyone can contribute to solutions.

6. *It is right to see challenging behaviour as just behaviour, not evidence of a pathological problem.* Challenging behaviour happens. Challenging behaviour grows out of small moments but can escalate quickly. Before we know it, challenging behaviour can become habitual – it seems so much an inherent part of the person it is easy to believe it is not learned. We each have the capacity to learn new ways of avoiding things or getting the things we need or want. Knowing what influences challenging behaviour is key to knowing how to pre-empt, support, respond or teach alternatives for the person. If we do not know why a given behaviour is happening, we might easily respond in a way that makes it worse. Finally, try not to take the behaviour personally. (It is unlikely the person is acting as they do simply to annoy you.)

7. *It is right to involve families and for families to receive high-quality advice and active support.* It is wrong to make families feel inadequate and unqualified to speak on behalf of the children they love. Some of the most insightful views and solutions come from those paid the least – support staff, teaching assistants – or even nothing at all (parents). It is right to work in partnership with people, even if you think someone is an utter arsehole.[1] (Arseholes may hold invaluable knowledge and insights, though the manner in which they express themselves is often difficult to stomach.) Remember, even arseholes have their uses (Sutton, 2010).

---

[1] If you are offended by inclusion of the A word then I can only apologise. When working for change in how children and adults with IDD whose behaviour challenges are understood and supported, I suspect far more offensive experiences will be encountered, such as exclusion, discrimination, sexual, financial, emotional and physical abuse, over-medication, restraint and indifference. Judicious use of a profanity is the least of the challenges we face.

8. *It is right to challenge any approach that dehumanises others.* It is right to challenge discrimination arising from challenging behaviour. Good support avoids punishment, good support builds skills such as communication, good support grows opportunities and belonging, and good support increases quality of life whilst decreasing loneliness and isolation. Good support writes new stories with people and questions severe reputations. Good support enables people to write their own stories.

9. Finally, A Brief Bill of Wrongs:

   – It is wrong to not have a shot at a good life.

   – It is wrong to have things taken away, to be hurt or made to feel unsafe.

   – It is wrong to be made to feel bad about yourself.

   – It is wrong for others to arbitrarily control the things you value.

   – It is wrong not be involved in your life decisions.

   – It is wrong to have your human rights revoked.

   – It is wrong to not fix unsuitable environments.

   – It is wrong to be told you cannot learn.

   – It is wrong not to be able to contribute.

   – It is wrong not to challenge challenging behaviour: it is wrong to accept it as inevitable.

KEY POINTS FROM *MANIFESTO: A BILL OF RIGHTS (AND WRONGS)*

- Human rights do not stop because challenging behaviour begins.
- It is right to be supported in person-centred and evidence-based ways.
- It is right to be consulted about how support is delivered.

CHAPTER 3

Working Together or Pulling Apart?

Coming together to discuss issues openly is an opportunity to share experiences, perspectives and solutions. No single person or group holds all knowledge. Challenging behaviour is difficult to deal with when you are alone: this is everything to do with the uncertainty such behaviour causes. The two following 'letters' illustrate the common frustrations that over the years I've heard expressed by professionals and parents. The only way forward is to work together.

About Professionals: A Letter to Families

Dear Family,

I have no magic wand. I'm a limited resource in high demand. Like undertakers or midwives, I will never be out of a job. My time is of the essence. My employers measure my effectiveness in terms of the number of people I advise whereas families measure me by the quality of the advice I give and my availability. I'm doomed to disappoint someone.

The first thing to go when I unpacked my training and began work in the real world was my capacity to spend time. I had to ration myself. All too often my job doesn't allow me to do what I once thought the job would be. I thought I'd have more autonomy to use my skills. (It feels wholly ironic to call ourselves a service at times, because we're increasingly expected to serve the interests of our own organisation.)

What you often want is my presence – in person or via a phone. You understandably want to feel supported, perhaps even not wholly alone. But I can't fix everything. I know it frustrates you when I fall into professional-speak, or say 'I know how you feel' even though I probably have no experience equal to your own, but that's how I'm trained, even though I suspect such trite phrases actually show a lack empathy. You've noticed I stopped talking of *cases* or *subjects*. That's an improvement.

There's an aspect of the professional's life that rightly dominates: accountability. I have to record everything in triplicate. There's a culture of fear that easily grows along with paperwork: if something goes wrong and my name is the last recorded point of contact, what I did and who I am will be questioned. I could be hung out to dry. Thank goodness we professionals are rarely held to account.

We have no magic solution. This is why often my colleagues and I prefer to be distant and indifferent, because we'd rather be a little impersonal than devastated. I can't fix disability and I can't mend broken hearts or marriages. (Though I can make a referral.)

I'm sorry if it feels to you that I expect crumbs from the captain's table to suffice. It makes me feel crumby, too. I can seek to mend the barriers to good person-centred work by challenging how we organise things, but you know what hierarchies are like. (They make us all stupid.) I can work to give you what you need rather than simply manage your expectations. I can be honest and try to not speak in a strange language at you. Finally, I can learn to pass on to you freely what my training and experience, my clinical intuition, have taught me, because you need these ideas each day.

When you ask me what you should be doing, perhaps out of self-doubt or fear, perhaps out of respect for my reputation, my job role or my qualification, I have learned to say, 'I'm sorry, I haven't a clue. I don't know the person. Not yet. But together we might come up with some ideas.'

About Families: A Letter to Professionals

Dear Professional,

We know you're busy so will keep this letter short and sweet, a little like your attention. Thanks for asking how we're doing. That stopped us in our tracks. We're so caught up in doing everyday things well – it feels we have to be better than any other family, just to pass muster – that when you asked us, we laughed. We hope you were not offended. Such questions are rare – time is an endangered species in your world – and it surprised us to hear someone in your position ask how we are doing as a couple and as a family.

Have you seen the signs at the train station that warn commuters to 'mind the gap'? We've joked about putting that sign on our front door. This family is moving at colossal speed and each appointment with professionals feels like a sudden stop to let a passenger join us for a moment. Mind the gap. Off we go.

We're very grateful for our child; we get tired and irritable: we become frustrated trying to get people to keep their promises and make human decisions, and we're sorry if you seem to get it in the ear. We've been waiting for the things you said we should experience – trauma and the 'bereavement of disability', but eleven years in and we're tired and (sometimes) a little beaten but we are not out and certainly do not regret the gift that is our fierce and beautiful daughter. I know she's difficult not to hear but she's easy to ignore.

What we want – as a family – is us: warts and all, challenging behaviour and disability. We'd like more time for us to be together, but who wouldn't? What we want *from you* is for you to be able to stand by us. We want you to be able to listen and pull us up short or give us advice when we need it. We want neither rocket science answers nor vagueness, neither critiques nor hints of wrongdoing. Talk to us normally. Be honest. No side-stepping, no avoidance. We want practical help when we need it: perhaps another pair of hands, a holiday, time for the other kids. We want to be able to speak to a competent someone when we need practical advice, or when we want to celebrate successes, or share our fears, or say *this is a bit shit right now.*

We sense the potential for us to fall into isolation. The very people whose job it is to make life easier often make it harder because of the way they work. Sometimes it feels the education system is designed to frustrate *everybody*. I'm sure you meet utterly horrible people. And some of them are in families and some are in professions.[1] This is too important to make much of personal affronts. Get over yourself and get off our case, get on our side.

The last time we met you had a student with you. We were asked if there was anything we would like to tell him. Tell him we'll welcome him based on his value to us as a family not because of his qualification. Respect has to be earned with each visit and with every letter. Respect is not awarded in perpetuity along with his doctorate. When he finishes his studies tell him that he will be a centaur: a half human and half professional creature that parents and people with intellectual disabilities will rely on. Tell him to remember that ultimately it is we – our daughter and her parents – who pay his ridiculous salary.

Tell him that numbers are important but it is stories people learn from. Loving someone whose behaviour challenges is hard but also joyful: what he does can make or break us. Tell him he will be privileged to hear our stories. A child with a disability is a child with a future, and a family with a child with disabilities is always a family: we will never stop being our daughter's parents. Love does not disappear come diagnosis.

Tell him that what he counts may not count with us. What matters to families may not matter to his bosses when they measure his impact. This *will* lead to differences of opinions. He needs to learn not to take offence: he represents a sometimes heartless system. He needs to take it on the chin. He needs to 'mind the gap'. Tell him to remember that it takes families a lot to ask for help, but it takes very little for him to screw trust up.

Tell him that despite the promises of inclusive education and community care, discovering a person-centred professional who knows their stuff still counts as a remarkable event. Tell him the small things that matter for children and adults with disabilities are only small to him; to us they make a significant difference. Tell him we are the experts: he is just someone who knows stuff. He doesn't know us.

---

1   The proportion of awful parents matches the proportion of awful professionals (Clements, 2013).

Tell him to come to our house at 9pm when things are not going well. Tell him to visit us at 4.30am when our daughter is up with the larks and laughing at the pillows tumbling over our heads. Tell him to sit with her when she is screaming and frightened by a world she does not understand, and the cruelty she experiences every day from people who should know better. Tell him life is not just or fair, and tell him not to add to the injustice. And if he can bring us a cup of coffee on his way up, he will be most welcome.

Tell him to remember our daughter has a name; she is fully qualified as a human and she is very much loved. And she loves us fiercely.

KEY POINTS FROM *WORKING TOGETHER OR PULLING APART?*

- Challenging behaviour is often difficult for one person to understand.

- Sharing our knowledge with others requires us to trust them.

- Not only must we feel we are taken seriously, we must take others seriously.

- Solutions are often negotiated from different perspectives.

- A busy professional can often come across as not listening.

- A busy family can often be perceived as challenging, when all they really want is good support.

CHAPTER 4

Behaviour is Lawful even when Awful

Exotic Communication

Communication plays such a vital role in our lives we often overlook it: like air, communication is both ubiquitous and invisible. We can easily become communicatively complacent, taking it for granted.

We can grow an understanding with people with whom we share a common code or language: we use it to share our ideas and ourselves. If we do not share a common code there is a gulf between us and we can easily misinterpret intentions and meanings. No doubt many of us have met people who talk in unfamiliar languages. Immediately we find ourselves at a disadvantage. What *do* they mean? We might begin to feel isolated or angry. Even if the code sounds familiar, subtle variations in meaning can cause confusion. Communication is a set of skills like any other, and like any other skill, people use communication skills to obscure, lie, bully and blame, as well as share their thoughts and feelings.

For most day-to-day encounters, we have a rough idea of what we each mean. Even when our words are jumbled we hope 'you know what I mean'. For many people with IDD, or those profoundly impacted by autism, conventional language does not develop without support: the number of people who do not have or use verbal communication is significant. The opportunities for confusion and mayhem are not to be under-estimated. It follows that many individuals inhabit the same physical but a different social world, drowned in words and fast communications, symbolism and subtle meanings that are only accessible if taught. Formal language is a code, the sounds a symbol of shared concepts. Sugar doesn't make the tongue sweet but those who know sugar understand what is meant.

Fortunately humans are a wildly talented bunch of primates and we do not have to rely solely on formal language. Other symbolic communications exist: a person can learn to sign or use pictures or symbols. Many of us use symbolic communication codes to share or obscure our intent or meanings. A good many of us use 'non-symbolic' methods, too, and these 'radiate' from us to others: body language, gestures and facial expressions. In other words, behaviour.

Children communicate before they speak and adults communicate without speaking, too. So *any* behaviour might start as unintentional – it is not *intended* to communicate anything at all – but over time, based on the responses gained, we can shape up these behaviours to mean something. By being together, we can grow meaning – subtle, nuanced or obvious – from almost any behaviour. This is why good friends can hold a private 'conversation' in the midst of wider gatherings with a look or gesture or code. Communication, then, is an exchange, a transmission of self.

A communication exchange requires at least two entities: the ebb and flow of interactions between people grow meanings through trial and error. When my children were babies they did not *intend* for me to pick them up and comfort them when they first cried – they just cried in response to physical discomfort such as hunger or being cold – but I interpreted their behaviour to mean they needed my attention and, more importantly, action. I made sure they were fed, cleaned and warmed. Why? Not simply because I am wonderful, but because doing so brought about a rapid end to their crying. They soon learned that crying results in a response. Twenty years later, I am somehow speaking to them about boyfriends, climate change, the ridiculous cost of higher education and the meaning of life according to Buddha. Early human exchanges and learning escalate *really* quickly like a compound interest of skills.

Those early foundational principles – you matter to me so I respond – are the bedrock of later skills as well as trust and rapport. If I *had not* responded to my children's unintentional behaviours – crying – I dread to think what would have happened to them or myself. The important principle to take from this is that learning to influence our surroundings often happens informally: before formal codes of communication develop we need informal *non-intentional* behaviours to occur.

If we are not paying attention we cannot respond, and early non-intentional behaviours will not be shaped. If individuals or infants do not receive a response their communication behaviour is extinguished – it stops. Nurturing the ebb and flow of interactions is vital. We do this by including our children in the realm of things that matter. Communication is very much an act of compassion.

If accidental or reflexive behaviour (an eye gaze, a cough, a cry of pain, a sneeze or blink) is viewed as *potentially* able to create a communication code (a blink means *this,* a cough *that,* a cry *something else*), we respond accordingly by investing time and interest. Meanings can then blossom. A positive reinforcement cycle can develop: behaviour is shown, we respond, the child responds to our responses, we respond to their response to our response... and soon we are growing together, weaving a tapestry of behaviours that become communication. Behaviour, speech and language are a choreography crafted from simple beginnings that grow in complexity and nuanced meaning. A baby goes *goo,* a toddler utters *doggy,* a child says *spaniel* because the people around them, through their responding, shape up verbal behaviour. We imbibe the ideas of others from the cot to the grave.

As children become better communicators tantrums tend to decrease. We each can have our moments when our communication is not heard or is misread but on the whole we give up crying for attention once we have learned more effective ways of securing attention. This is because our repertoire of skills grows as we develop. But some children with IDD and some autistic children do not develop these skills so easily. Where communication abilities have not been developed in children we often see higher rates of challenging behaviours. It appears then that those with poor communication skills, or who are in environments not sensitive to the need to shape up behaviours to act as communication, are more likely to show behaviour considered challenging.

The Communication Hypothesis

The communication hypothesis (Carr *et al.*, 1994) suggests challenging behaviour 'often functions as a primitive form of communication for those individuals who do not yet possess or use more sophisticated forms of communication that would enable them to influence others to obtain a variety of desirable outcomes' (p.22). It is important to remember that no one is suggesting a person who does not speak will be doomed to display behaviour that challenges; only that there are likely to be more opportunities for communication to not develop or be missed. It will simply take more work for early skills to blossom into complex communicative behaviours. It is important to remember that people who do communicate well are also quite able to show behaviours that may be considered challenging. Finally, no one suggests people whose behaviour is termed challenging intentionally use their behaviour to influence others. There is little evidence that challenging behaviour is *intended* to make your life difficult.

The communication hypothesis is a metaphor to use when we seek to understand challenging behaviour: do not think of challenging behaviour as a pathological issue we need to eliminate; think of it as being like a potential communication. The communication hypothesis asks us to wonder: what might this mean?

The communication hypothesis means we can start thinking of legitimate ways to hear the person's message better. We can work to support the individual to learn that communicating in a way more people recognise – a sign, a word, a symbol – is more effective than challenging behaviour.

We teach by responding consistently to people in certain ways. This is a constructive exchange and growing of meaning.

The communication hypothesis suggests we can benefit from thinking of self-injury, aggression and other challenging behaviours as saying something to us. If someone is hurting themselves whenever they are asked to do an activity, it would be better for them to learn to say, sign or show another way of communicating, 'I don't want to do this activity.' If we teach communication skills to the person and those around them we often reduce challenging behaviour whilst increasing the autonomy of the person with IDD. The key processes are:

- Identify the message (or function) of the challenging behaviour. (Does the individual regularly gain attention, a preferred item, or sensory feedback, or do they escape or avoid people or things, following the behaviour?)

- Identify a communication method that is quicker and takes less effort than the challenging behaviour, and that guarantees the same outcome is achieved.

- Ensure those around the individual can deliver the outcome quickly and consistently.

- The 'new' communication mode competes with the challenging behaviour: being quicker and taking less effort it is likely to be used more than the challenging behaviour.

You can see this approach works best for behaviours with functions that are clearly shown to be what is called socially mediated – they involve others. Attention is socially mediated (someone has to give attention), as is escape from people (the person goes away), escape from a task (the task is removed), and getting a preferred, tangible item (often someone provides the item or facilitates its delivery). Challenging behaviour sends us a message and finding less harmful ways to send the same message underpins many support programmes.

To illustrate the importance of assuming behaviour has meaning, let us meet Nancy.

Nancy is a young woman profoundly impacted by IDD and health issues. She has a supportive family who have organised services in such a way that she lives in her own home where she has regular staff as well as family members taking oversight. Nancy doesn't speak but can vocalise and has only three consistent signs she uses: 'please', 'more' and 'no'. In the last six months Nancy has been seen to hurt herself more often – specifically, she hits the side of her head against the kitchen worktop. This is intense and frightening; Nancy has attended hospital ten times in the last half year.

The communication hypothesis says we might better support Nancy if we assume this self-harming behaviour is telling us something. People began to gather information to look for clues about the 'message'. They found:

- Nancy is likely to hit her head when asked to complete a cooking task she is not familiar with.

- The new microwave seemed to be not as clear as the broken model it replaced and this featured in many incidents of self-harm.

- It tended to be newer staff still undergoing their induction who were supporting Nancy when she hurt herself.

- It became clear Nancy was agitated for an hour or so before these events – her face was a little scrunched up, her vocalisations louder than normal, and she was seen to be pulling the earlobe of her right ear.

The communication hypothesis suggested that Nancy's behaviour might mean: 'I am in pain. I don't understand the new microwave. And I'm not keen on how the new person is supporting me.'

In response a doctor's appointment found Nancy had a significant ear infection. This was treated and within a few days people reported a reduction in agitation. People noticed Nancy was able to concentrate on learning about the new microwave. Time was spent teaching: demonstrating, then guiding, and finally sign-prompting Nancy to use the controls.

Nancy's self-harm reduced to once every fortnight, but this coincided with one particular newer staff member supporting her. The staff and family took a closer look at how Nancy was supported during these times. They discovered the newer staff member had not been inducted into the nuances of responding to Nancy's early warning signs that she was unhappy: this meant the new staff member did not respond when Nancy asked for a break from the new cooking task she was being shown. Staff felt Nancy's self-harm was saying, 'I don't understand what this new person is asking.'

The staff group reworked its own practices concerning inductions to avoid these issues. The new staff member was coached through role-play and conversation about how best to support Nancy, and how to read the 'early warning signs' things were not going so well for her. But because Nancy had learned not to trust this new staff member as much as others, the family and staff decided to hide (or embed) the new learning he was teaching Nancy in a more fun activity. In effect doing so 'reset' their relationship by focusing on rapport building.

Beyond the intervention focusing on staff support, the family and staff team thought a more thorough examination of communication would be helpful to guide how they support Nancy. With the support of a speech therapist they were able to understand:

- Most communication to Nancy was verbal yet it was shown Nancy could confidently respond to two or three key words in each sentence. Too much verbal communication predicted misunderstanding. The newer staff tended to use more words.

- Nancy seemed to get more information from the context than verbal communication. Nancy knew what to do when being asked to warm drinks or heat meals in the old microwave despite staff talking. When the new microwave was bought Nancy could not immediately see how to open the door or set the timer. It was new and confusing. Staff talking too much simply added to the muddle.

- Staff relearned what they had forgotten through familiarity: Nancy relies on a few key words, gestures and signing, and contexts, in order to understand. Nancy used to sign a lot more, but because new staff had not been trained to sign, signing became less used. The staff were taught to sign Nancy's preferred signs by the home leader and Nancy: they did this when supporting Nancy in their day-to-day work.

- To maintain skills, staff meetings had an expectation that staff would speak and sign rather than talk.

- A 'communication passport' was begun: a passport helps us travel toward understanding. For Nancy, the five-sheet passport contained symbols and pictures and outlined methods of communication for staff, examples of how not to do it and examples of how to do it (Millar and Aitkin, 2003).

For Nancy, there is a recognition that challenging behaviour is not her fault or responsibility. It is not pathological but a message. It is the responsibility of us all to do something about interpreting it and responding positively.

Exotic Communication

Geraint Ephraim argued that there are two kinds of psychologists: the talkers and the doers. The doers are pragmatic and optimistic simultaneously (no mean feat) and they achieve this by providing practical ideas that are suitable for people given their circumstances. Ephraim left us a rich endowment of enthusiasm and suggestions concerning how to understand and support people with IDD and autistic people as well as their staff and families.

Ephraim's primary contribution to my practice was a brief chapter he wrote in 1998. Ephraim suggested that no ifs and no buts about it, behaviour *was* communication. He argued that challenging behaviour, as we often think of it, simply does not exist. What we take for challenging behaviour is actually 'exotic communication'. We always respond to such behaviour (Ephraim, 1998) because a physical or verbal assault is not something we can ignore: '…there is no such thing as challenging behaviour. What we have is exotic communication… A punch in the face is an act of communication which is very difficult not to hear. Its effect may be heard but the message behind the punch may not have been listened to, let alone understood' (Ephraim, 1998, pp.211–12).

Ephraim suggested people think of communication as a parcel of information that they fling at one another. When it is flung at a person who does not comprehend the language we use we blame them for our inability to fling a parcel using the language they are able to catch. Ephraim argued that we should try to learn (and teach) a common language. He argued that hurling parcels is not as useful as having an equal conversation based on a shared code.

Too many interactions end in the livid throwing back and forth of parcels that are less communication, more weapon. Instead of a conversation that is mutually respectful we can end up in a struggle for control, and where such struggles dominate the narrative we find exotic communication. Ephraim warns his reader that, 'where there is denial of the other's uniqueness, there is no conversation' (1998, p.223). Ephraim argued that exotic communication is an expensive way to deliver not a very good life. He recommended investing in mutually respectful conversations, which saves money and is more likely to contribute to everybody's happiness. Ephraim shows the vital importance of taking people seriously as communicators worthy of being heard.

Exotic communication is a helpful motif because it is an easy way to comprehend the implications of the communication hypothesis. If we were to write a recipe to promote exotic communication we might take the dry ingredients of not bothering to understand the experiences of the person we are spending time with, add a pinch of thinking we do not *need* to learn their language, stir in an element of under- or over-estimating the person, before finally mixing with the oil of believing the job at hand is to tell people what to do. Place in boiling water for ten minutes, stand back, and watch the show. Ephraim warns his reader that if we fail to accept one another's unique way of communicating it will be impossible to have a meaningful conversation. He shows that everyone deserves to be heard, and hearing saves a lot of heartache.

It does not take much to foster exotic communication because it is hard to take people seriously when we believe we are better than them or that their voices do not count because of a label. We can change what we do in light of what we think the behaviour is 'saying' but how we interpret the message of the behaviour is utterly dependent on us taking the person seriously enough to assume their behaviour can tell us something.

Ephraim finished his brief chapter by suggesting we extend our knowledge about challenging behaviour to families. If we fail to listen to families we are not taking them seriously and we will not promote a conversation, only exotic communication. Too often too many families feel marginalised and at the edges of the provision they are entitled to. Being excluded from what should be ours by right is likely to make us all exotic communicators.

If we do not take the person seriously we will fail to listen in a way that can take meaning from behaviour. We will then do what all robots do and simply assume the individual does not compute or make any sense. We will do what we are programmed to do: ignore, reprimand, walk away, blame or shout, and become authoritarian toward families and their children. We do these things only if we assume the person does not matter, is unworthy of being heard, and their behaviour is a product of their disability. This approach – known as a pathological approach – implies there's no point in listening to what the behaviour is saying because what it is saying does not matter because the person does not matter. We all know what this feels like when a manager or professionals uses jargon. They throw parcels *intentionally* over our heads then blame us for not catching their meaning.

And so we will employ more and more drastic behaviours in complaint. In so doing we lose sight of the humanity of the person who is throwing parcels, so we aim a few parcels back. And this is how we slowly lose our own humanity and end up being exotic communicators ourselves. By not listening to others, we run the risk of becoming like those people throwing parcels that we dislike so very much.

KEY POINTS CONCERNING *EXOTIC COMMUNICATION*

- Challenging behaviour carries a message.
- This message is legitimate even if the behaviour is harmful or dangerous or considered 'not appropriate'.
- When and where the behaviour most often occurs gives us clues about what the message means.
- Communication is a two-way street: listening means changing how we think about the person, their behaviour, and most importantly, what we do in response to the person's behaviour.

Behaviour is Lawful even when Awful

Challenging behaviour might be helpfully thought of as having meaning because these behaviours often rely on the responses of others, either to fetch something, stop something or provide attention. Challenging behaviour tells *us* something about the person's health, happiness or needs.

Research into challenging behaviour owes much of its robustness to the paradigms underpinning applied behaviour analysis (ABA). ABA posits human behaviour can be better understood when we identify what is termed 'functional relationships' – how one thing follows another.

Behaviour does not occur in isolation from anything else. Behaviour is correlated with other events in the person or outside of the person: behaviour is made more likely (or predicted) by certain events, and behaviour always achieves an outcome. A functional relationship might read as follows: *when she is interrupted watching a film on television, and is prompted to clean her room, Carrie is likely to shout, a result of which is her father helping her clean.* Typically we call the process of exploring functional relationships a functional assessment.

To understand what predicts a behaviour occurring we examine regular events that occur before the behaviour. The things that happen before behaviour are called antecedents or predictors. An antecedent is a signal that indicates behaviour is likely to be followed by a certain outcome. For example when driving, a red light at a road crossing is an antecedent to braking. The consequence of my braking is I do not crash (or get fined by police). (Staying alive is a fairly fundamental reinforcer.)

We cannot assume a reinforcer for behaviour in one person is transferrable to another behaviour or person. Not all of us work for pay but we all work for something. A reinforcer is individual: some people find chocolate pleasurable, others do not. Some people enjoy attention, others not. And some will find the exhilaration of driving fast through a red light reinforcing. So for them a red light signals a chance to drive fast and feel fortunately amazed at their survival, or bask in the adoration of admirers. It may be antisocial but even antisocial can be reinforcing for some people due to their histories.

This is the basic pattern of behaviour then: *Antecedents (Predictors)* signal *Behaviour* will be reinforced by a *Consequence*. This pattern is known as the three-term contingency. The consequence tells us a good deal about the function of the behaviour – what the person gains or avoids.

We'll explore how we establish the function (the consequence) of any given behaviour in the chapter on 'Exploring' (Chapter 6).

The three-term contingency is incredibly useful even if it is not wholly correct. (It is not wholly incorrect either: it is simply not the whole story.)

A significant issue worth mentioning is that there are actually two broad *types* of antecedent or predictor events that make a given behaviour more likely: the immediate antecedent predictor and earlier factors that influence our susceptibility to the immediate predictor.

My walking into a shop to buy a sandwich is influenced not by a sign advertising sandwiches but whether I am hungry. When I am not hungry the sign has no effect. Thus hunger is a *fourth* contingency and is known as a setting event (though other terms have been associated with similar influences on behaviour, for example 'motivating operation' and 'establishing operation'). Setting events can include the presence of something (such as an illness), as well as the absence of something (such as a lack of attention). Think of setting events as motivators that change what we want.

We can then modify the three-term contingency to a four-term contingency: *Setting Events (Motivators)* alter the reinforcing potential of the *Antecedents (Predictors)*, thus affecting the likelihood of *Behaviour* because they signal likely *Consequences*. We'll return to the amazing possibilities of these two antecedents for supporting people better in later chapters. The illustration below shows how these contingencies might work together (Table 4.1).

Table 4.1: Contingency Example

Antecedents (before the behaviour)		Behaviour	Consequences
Setting events: 'motivators'	Predictors	What the person does	Outcomes
Things that affect the 'power' of the predictor	The signal that behaviour may be reinforced	The action	What follows: attention, escape, tangible, sensory
Tony is hungry	Tony sees the fridge	Tony opens fridge and eats something	Tony is not hungry (Tony escapes hunger, gets sensory satisfaction)

In terms of consequences, we believe we can summarise all consequences into four simplistic categories or groups: human behaviour has only four broad functions or outcomes:

- behaviours that gain social attention

- behaviours that gain tangible items

- behaviours that ensure avoidance or escape

- behaviours that provide or avoid sensory feedback.

It is important to make explicit that the above functions are intentionally broad categories: more nuanced and individualised functions are the actual product of person-centred functional assessments. It would be simple if one behaviour *always* achieved the same consequences, but much behaviour achieves different outcomes depending on where, when and with whom they occur.

For example, writing this book was multi-functional (it did not result in one outcome). At one level, writing this book provided me with a tangible item: a book I kept promising myself I would write when I was old enough to almost know what I was talking about. At another level the book felt good to write (so a sensory function), and I guess I would have written it whether it resulted in publication as a book or not. At another level writing the book let me escape other work demands. Finally, some people gave me attention whilst I was writing it. So you can see that writing was multi-functional. For other people, writing a book would have many different functions.

These categories of attention, escape, tangible and sensory are very broad categories indeed. A more person-centred assessment would tell us what kind of work demands (or people) I escaped whilst writing, and what precisely the sensory feedback I received from writing it was (a sense of achievement, an endorphin jolt, the peace and quiet of writing, a long overdue promise finally delivered to someone I love by writing this book, thus helping me escape a vague unease at letting that person down…and so forth).

So why do we adhere to such broad categories of functions of behaviour? Simply because knowing someone wants attention, even if we're still working on what that precisely looks like, allows us to start exploring the giving of attention immediately. Broad categories of function allow us to look at interventions quickly that are at least in the right functional area. We can hone our understanding and tailor how precisely to deliver nuanced support as we go: our understanding of function and influences on behaviour is an iterative process, and not fixed.

And so we can say behaviour is lawful even when awful. Knowing there is an explanation for behaviour hidden away or in plain sight helps us know how better to support and respect the individual's preferences. While the above knowledge is drawn from extensive scientific research, our application of the science should be informed, as Ephraim noted, by a conversation with those who will need to apply that knowledge every day. Every moment offers opportunities to avoid exotic communication and promote a conversation. It helps to know that we are speaking the same language.

KEY POINTS CONCERNING *BEHAVIOUR IS LAWFUL EVEN WHEN AWFUL*

- Challenging behaviour is meaningful for the individual even if it is confusing for others.

- Using person-centred approaches can help us understand the person's preferences.

- Quality of life matters to all of us.

- To reduce challenging behaviour we need to change lifestyles and relationships.

- To reduce challenging behaviours we need to teach new ways of doing things.

- A mosaic of small interventions is often better than a single intervention.

- We should aim to fix the ecology, not aim to fix the person.

What does All This Result In?

If challenging behaviour can be thought of as communication, two things follow. First, through understanding when behaviour happens and what follows it we can describe a 'best guess' as to what the message of the behaviour is. It might say 'I want attention, an end to this, a thing, a feeling.' We do not need to speak to communicate. Second, we should cease to focus on seeking ways to stop behaviour but rather either:

- 'shape' it into a form of communication recognised by many, or

- come up with an alternative behaviour that competes with the challenging behaviour.

If we do not know the answer to the first we will struggle to achieve the second. If we do not consider challenging behaviour as exotic communication we will not attempt to communicate.

As Ephraim wisely warned us, if we do not have a conversation we will start shouting and end up battling over who matters the most. Communication, then, is an exchange, a sharing.

To be effective, communication needs to be enabled by the ecology and by each other. We do this by having a communication-friendly environment (not too loud, not too many distractions) and ensuring people are clear how to respond and present information. A communication strategy will fail miserably unless people around the child or adult respond consistently. To respond consistently we need to ensure people take the individual seriously and view them as someone who matters.

In terms of teaching alternatives to challenging behaviour we can ask one simple question: is there a different behaviour that takes less energy than the challenging behaviour? This is why one simple question to ask people is 'What could the person do instead of the challenging behaviour?'

The *key* principle for intervention is this: does the *alternative* behaviour have the same outcome as the challenging behaviour? If it does, the *alternative* behaviour is said to be functionally equivalent. This is an important principle as it makes the new behaviour perhaps easier to learn. Because it is important we will return to it again later in the book.

Recap Before Moving On

What we have learned so far is that thinking about challenging behaviour as meaningful and potentially communicative is a significant change that can bring considerable benefits (Halle, 1994).

We have suggested challenging behaviour is in part a social construction. It is very real and impactful but people construct the meaning. If we 'reframe' how we think about challenging behaviour not as a problem to be stopped but as an exotic communication to be understood, we find ourselves one step closer to adopting what have been called 'upstream solutions'.

A rather wonderful parable explains upstream solutions:

> The story goes that a person walking alongside a river sees someone drowning. This person jumps in, pulls the victim out, and begins artificial respiration. While this is going on, another person calls for help; the rescuer jumps into the water again and pulls the new victim out. This process repeats itself several times until the rescuer gets up and walks away from the scene. A bystander approaches and asks in surprise where he is going, to which the rescuer replies 'I'm going upstream to find out who's pushing all these people in and see if I can stop it!' (Egan and Cowan, 1979, pp.3–4)

This parable is an immensely powerful teaching story because those parts of Serviceland that are intended to support children or adults with IDD, or who work to support autistic people whose behaviour challenges others, are innately *downstream* solutions to *upstream* problems. They are constantly trying to save people from the river, whereas expertise should be turning off the supply of people early on. This is why in a way challenging behaviour is partly a public health issue.

Waiting until challenging behaviour develops before offering preventative strategies is not that sensible when you think about it. Hence the recent focus in research on very early interventions to support families and children. At an individual level if we respond as powerfully to the person *before* challenging behaviour as we do *after* it, we might save everyone a lot of heartache.

Upstream solutions can be applied to individuals on a day-to-day basis in that we can avoid or amend situations that often lead to challenging behaviour, and we can think of applying such an approach to lifetimes: teach a child early the skills they need to meet their needs, avoid a world of future pain. We do this ourselves each time we decide to get fit, or change our diets, or give up smoking. It is helpful to remember we can adopt a similar approach to our relationships with others, because our lives, our thinking, our behaviour, are all the results of our lives, our thinking, our behaviour from yesterday, last week, last month, last year…

KEY POINTS FROM THIS CHAPTER

- Communication is functional – it achieves something.
- Challenging behaviour is likewise functional – it achieves something.
- We can think of challenging behaviour as telling us something.
- The communication hypothesis doesn't suggest all challenging behaviour is intentionally communicative but we can interpret it as such.
- Regular, everyday and interesting activities and exchanges help set the scene for learning how to communicate with one another.
- Behaviour is learned through interactions, therefore challenging behaviour is not just an issue in the person, but a responsibility of us all.
- People often not only rely on the good communication skills of others but on their human values and their respect.
- If you do not enjoy the challenging behaviour and wish it would stop, you need to know what the person gets from it and discover how else the person might get the same thing but from an alternative behaviour that's quicker and easier to do.

Don't Lose Your Human

The book has several 'Keeping Your Human Well-Nourished' vignettes (or little illustrations) that show precisely what it looks like when we endeavour to keep sight of the bigger picture surrounding challenging behaviour. They show what is required to see the person first, and to keep behaviour in context. They are examples of our *shared* role as guardians of humanity in an all too commonly robot-festooned human service system. Let us begin by considering broad principles.

Most of the people you meet were born as remarkably tiny humans. These tiny humans needed constant nourishment to grow into larger humans, but life is hectic and sometimes through no fault of their own some tiny humans miss meals and can whither into something resembling a robot rather than a larger human. You can spot a robot because they're not so good at listening: they expect others to reply in ways very much like a script. Robots are terribly keen to follow protocols, orders and policies at the expense of the happiness of other humans. Robots are a little angular, whereas humans come in *all* shapes.

The other thing you'll notice about robots is their obsession with data and numbers. It's almost as if humans get in the way of their careful plans. Robots like humans to live in boxes: support worker, teacher, parent, service user – each with clearly defined roles and limitations. Indeed, robots have produced hundreds of such boxes, and everyone has to fit into one. If you straddle two boxes you just confuse robots, because robots don't do Venn diagrams. Robots have been conditioned to believe the Beatles were wrong: all you need is *not*

love – all you need is the graphical depiction of data. There are times robots won't believe anything you say unless you speak in numbers. It is possible to remind robots of their original state as tiny humans, but they do not welcome it and can short-circuit or lash out if you ask them too many human questions such, 'What about friendships? What about happiness and belonging? Will my son or daughter be safe in your care?' Thank goodness there are thousands of humans at work in Serviceland resisting their robotic overlords.

Humans can be recognised because they tend to take a common-sense approach to those around them based on hard-to-compute things such as happiness and belonging. Humans, despite what you hear on the news, are characterised by compassion and a dry sense of humour. (In Serviceland, humour is as essential as oxygen.) A well-nourished human needs to spend time with other humans who listen and take people seriously, rather than viewing them as problems to be solved. Well-nourished humans will make use of the skills commonly found in robots without becoming robots themselves. Well-nourished humans can make use of technology without the technology taking them over. You can identify well-nourished humans by the way they speak to people, by the way they take others seriously, and by the fact they like to listen to stories other people tell. Well-nourished humans spend time wisely. They apply human solutions to human problems, and recognises practically everyone they meet is fairly similar to themselves whilst also being wonderfully unique, including (and here's the important point) robots. A well-nourished human tends to assume robots are little humans lost in the wonders of numbers. Humans know even robots have vestiges of tiny humans within them; robots simply need to be encouraged to regrow their human.

These days when reading books and articles and advice about Serviceland you would be forgiven for believing humans are an endangered species. There are lots of policies, hundreds of protocols, thousands of strategies; and funnily enough, many of these have been cut and pasted from *other* policies, protocols and strategies. But all of these managerial solutions need humans to make them work, to interpret statements and enact them. And what makes humans work well is less about policies and more about other humans. The good news is for every robot we encounter there are dozens of humans working hard to deliver a meaningful day to people *despite* the robots. These humans are often not in positions of authority because being a robot is a fairly good predictor of gaining a promotion.

> **KEY POINTS FROM *DON'T LOSE YOUR HUMAN***
>
> • It is terribly easy to refer to people as cases, subjects and disorders. Resist this and refer to people in a way they prefer.
>
> • Becoming a robot does your own career no harm, but can cause immensurable harm to the people who ultimately pay your salary.

Keeping Your Human Well-Nourished: Jane

Jane is an autistic young woman whose self-injury was dangerous to her own physical and emotional well-being. Even though dangerous, her self-injury was important to Jane – it is how she expressed herself. Self-injury was daily and intense, lasting up to three hours an episode. Jane would hit her face and forehead against taps and coat hooks and walls with such violence people could hear the impact next door. Staff were traumatised and fearful. To gain new clothes, Jane ripped her old clothes. To gain new toiletries, Jane poured away half-used ones.

Jane lived in a residential service that could not cope with the risks to Jane or her staff. One weekend Jane found herself in a small assessment unit holding an empty suitcase. She wore one hospital gown, had no clothes, no friendships, but she did have endless behaviour support plans written by psychologists. The plans were based on the assumption that Jane hurt herself to (a) get new clothes, and (b) gain attention from staff. The plan stated that when Jane hurt herself she would need to be restrained, and to avoid reinforcing the self-injury Jane was not allowed to wear her own clothes for a set period of time following self-injury. Hence the ever-ready hospital gowns. Jane ripped these to shreds periodically and could often be found walking around in a towel.

The interventions focused on extinction. Extinction programmes as applied to Jane meant not reinforcing her self-injury by giving her clothes or too much attention. Jane was not shown how to cope with her frustrations. The extinction programme seemed to *increase* challenging behaviour.

One support worker read the plans, spent time with a very angry and utterly frightened Jane, and let go her tiny human during an assessment unit team meeting. 'Why can't Jane have *her* clothes? Nowhere here does it say *why* Jane loves clothes! What they *mean* to Jane! Why must we take away from Jane the only thing she has? We can't take away anything from Jane that she can't take away from herself! Jane is taking away her own *face*! Why don't we give attention, clothes and anything Jane needs *before* self-injury? Jane shouldn't have to earn basic things in the name of therapy.'

The unit manager said he would discuss this with the clinical supervisor, the individual responsible for Jane's support. The trouble with robots is they think they have a God-given right to restrict access to things the rest of us take for granted, be that fun, laughter, friendship, clothing, honesty, communication and hope. Robots will find out the things you like, and make you earn them by doing what they want you to do. Robots figure choice is less important than you doing what they say you should do. Robots use the mantra 'We have a duty to care' as a euphemism for 'Follow the programme and you might earn your human rights back.'

Robots dissect and reduce humans in order to comprehend them: robots describe pathologies, disabilities, deficits and problems. If you read a document about someone you love and you cannot recognise the person, you can be fairly sure a robot following a script has written it. Jane did not follow a script: the services Jane experienced expected Jane to fit in with them.

Too often we parachute staff, parents, autistic persons, and adults with IDD into robotic services that are not fit for purpose. What works best is designing a service around the person's unique needs. What works best for staff is to be valued and supported themselves, not expected to act like robots.

In 2005 David Pitonyak wrote a paper that suggests there are ten human things we can do to support a person whose behaviour others find difficult. We can:

1. Get to know the person by spending time with them to discover what they like and do not like. Do more of the former, less of the latter.

2. Interpret the *meaning* of the behaviour. What the behaviour gets tells us if the individual:

   - feels alone

   - is bored

   - has few choices, less control, little power and lacks self-determination

   - doesn't feel safe

   - is not valued

   - is in pain or frustrated by their bodies or ill-health

   - is struggling to communicate other than through behaviour.

3. Involve the individual in creating the plan by asking what kind of life the person aspires to.

4. Develop a support plan for those supporting the person.

5. Assume nothing from the labels or reputation accompanying the person.

6. Be clear that it is relationships that make the difference.

7. Craft a positive identity with the person.

8. Give chances rather than ultimatums.

9. Maximise opportunities for enjoyment.

10. Develop a rapport with health or other professionals (Pitonyak, 2005).

Jane's support team did not invest in their own well-being and were exhausted. Their relationship with professionals was fraught with disagreements about the messages Jane was sending: this served to undermine their confidence. Jane's life had been stripped of enjoyment and she was not involved in her support planning. The support plans told people what could be withheld and withdrawn, and every good thing Jane wanted had to be earned. Jane spent much of her time alone – people kept a distance because they were afraid of the ferocity she showed. People and systems lacking imagination and empathy, with fixed interests and idiosyncratic communication, surrounded Jane. More than one person thought the way Jane was supported was evidently more autistic than Jane.

Asking human questions about Jane helps us see her better. Because it is terrible and all too easy to see things in a way that suggests Jane is a problem, her challenging behaviour defines her, and her diagnosis of autism is all that matters. These things are significant but they are far from being the only things that matters to Jane.

KEY POINTS FROM *KEEPING YOUR HUMAN WELL-NOURISHED: JANE*

- Jane speaks for herself, but not many can hear her.
- Who speaks for Jane if not you?
- Who keeps an eye out for what Jane needs if not you?
- Who can get to know Jane better than you?
- Who can become the one person Jane learns to trust if not you?
- If not you then who?
- If not now then when?

Introducing Franny: Learning to Listen

Let me introduce Franny. She is a young girl who will accompany us throughout the remainder of the book. Her story will illustrate the issues we consider. Franny is a composite character, taken from a myriad of real individuals.

The language we use to describe people is telling. In describing Franny we are describing primarily a child, not a case and not a subject. We are speaking of somebody's daughter, a person in her own right. When asked to support someone whose behaviour challenges others it is vital to see the human first, not a diagnosis.

Franny

Franny is nine years old. She attends a small mainstream school where academically she is doing well given the support provided. Franny's primary teacher is Mrs Irving and like many of her colleagues she has an enthusiasm for inclusive education. The school is led by a head teacher (Miss Neruda) who has a child with an IDD, so her leadership style is professional, passionate and *personal*. Socially, Franny is a little isolated, learning to rely more on her adult support than her peers. The school employs two learning-support assistants and Franny takes up a lot of their time. When asked, Franny made herself distinct from her classmates: 'The others are different. They don't like me.'

A paediatrician and an educational psychologist have been seeing Franny regularly for a few months now, and Franny's grandparents pay for both because they could not wait the eighteen months it takes statutory services to deliver appointments. This makes Franny very fortunate. Both the paediatrician and the educational psychologist agree Franny has a mild intellectual disability, probably attributed to a difficult labour where she was without oxygen for a while. This has been mitigated to some degree by the very active involvement of Franny's wider family. Franny is lucky as she has a rich network of people around her. However, the family is at risk of growing quite insular, having learned to rely on their own resources. In the last couple of years Franny's parents have begun the process of seeking a more detailed diagnosis for her, believing she shows clear signs of being autistic. Franny is funny ('sarcasm is her second language,' Mrs Irving notes) and has learned the benefits of making her classmates laugh.

Over the last few months, a word is beginning to be heard more and more often: autism. The school staff suggest Franny is not autistic but her parents are beginning to wonder. Franny has quite fixed ideas about how her days should go, and she has limited interests: sudden changes in routines really cause Franny problems. The paediatrician the family sometimes pay for is prepared to look into this in more detail, because she knows it is often younger girls who are missed when diagnosing autism. It is almost as if the diagnostic tests are better suited to boys not girls. The paediatrician has also told Franny's parents that given the disruption in her life recently, some of the autistic-like behaviours may have other causes.

Franny's parents separated two years ago. They have tried to remain on good terms and explain the situation to Franny. She spends Sunday to Wednesday with her mother Lynne in the original family home, Thursday to Saturday, with her father John ten miles away. Franny is an only child. Recently Franny's mother has started a new relationship with Molly, a long-time friend of the family, and Molly has moved in.

In the last year Franny started pinching herself at night in bed – her wrists, thighs and stomach are often bruised. Sometimes, she uses objects – old pens, a protractor, a dulled pair of scissors. Sometimes, Franny makes her skin bleed. This has been termed 'self-harm' and both parents are openly discussing it with Franny. Both parents are clearly upset and sometimes these discussions escalate into reprimands from John – even thoughtful fathers are overcome by fear when thinking about the safety of their daughters. Lynne has berated John in front of Franny about his 'telling off Franny', and that conversation was the first time Franny saw her parents argue and her father cry. 'I just want Franny to not need to hurt herself,' John says. 'And reprimanding her won't do that,' Lynne counters. 'Nothing I do is right by you,' John replied.

Both John and Lynne are speaking with a therapist using narrative approaches – both are rewriting the changes to their life stories, and sketching out their futures. So far this has gone well, but clearly both are more deeply impacted by Franny's diagnosis than they thought at the time. Their stories about the future are both hugely uncertain.

There have been times in the last two years when Franny has become 'incredibly angry' (Miss Neruda), 'frustrated with all the changes' (Mrs Irving), throwing herself to the floor and banging her head in class. The school calls this a 'meltdown' and are seeking advice about helping Franny to stay calm and cope with challenging situations. The school are waiting for a visit from an educational psychologist and the education authority's behaviour support service. In the meantime, they believe these meltdowns are about Franny escaping hard tasks, and about expressing her feelings. They encourage Franny to talk and to leave the class to calm down.

Franny's self-harm takes place mainly at her mother's. It is discovered only when her mother helps her get ready in the mornings. Franny tries to hide her injuries. It happens about three times a week on average at Franny's mother's but it does vary in intensity – sometimes light marks, sometimes heavy bruising, and sometimes bleeding – and if there is one day that *always* features self-harm it is a Wednesday. Franny also self-harms some nights at her father's new flat, but this is less common. 'Though he doesn't check as often as I do. He lets Franny get herself ready,' Lynne told the school. When Franny stays with her father no meltdowns have been seen. 'They happen a couple of times a week at her proper home,' Lynne reports.

School say they have experienced no major problems apart from meltdowns. Franny has begun to walk or run out of class (typically during some subjects more than others) and is usually found running around the athletics field. Teachers often encourage Franny to leave rather than have a meltdown. Teachers often fetch her back to class after ten minutes of running. 'Any sooner and Franny isn't ready,' Mrs Irving explains. It is said Franny will usually return to the task at hand. Franny has just been given a watch, and school want her to time herself in order to return to class after ten minutes.

QUESTIONS ABOUT *INTRODUCING FRANNY: LEARNING TO LISTEN*

- What are the significant events that might affect how Franny thinks, feels or behaves?

- Make a list of the different behaviours Franny shows that are causing concern, then answer:

- Do we know what seems to predict each?

- Do we know what Franny seems to get or avoid from these behaviours?

CHAPTER 5

The Elephants in the Room

On Being Person Centred

Before going on to examine how to establish *why* a particular behaviour is happening, there are some elephants in the room we need to identify, capture and relocate someplace they are not able to squish people.

You might think elephants would be pretty obvious to spot, especially in a small suburban two up two down, but elephants (it turns out) are tricky to catch sight of: people become habituated to the elephants in their living room and so fail to spot them. Elephants become invisible to many people working in Serviceland, it seems.

If you spot and then remove or tame these elephants you might not need more technical solutions to challenging behaviour. Seeing them requires standing back and taking a long look at what is all too familiar to you. Spotting elephants is harder than it sounds because elephants have learned to blend into the background. They adopt new names that make it easier for us to ignore them, names such as 'This Is Just The Way Life Is', and 'We Don't Have The Budget For Best Practice', and 'You're Not Paid To Think or Ask Embarrassing Questions'.

The amazing thing about canny elephants in the room is that they have learned to camouflage themselves despite their lack of opposable thumbs. Removing elephants can give us space to think differently about problems, and may even mean we will not need to call on expensive solutions to solve conundrums of behaviour.

To be person centred is to work to deliver the life the individual needs; being person centred is to ask human questions. For example, we might ask:

- Is the person well?

- Is the person living a good life?

- Are family or staff around the person being well supported?

Often challenging behaviour is a symptom of an unquiet life lived by someone at the margins of society. Being person centred means seeing the person as a whole person. Being person centred is an upstream solution. By addressing the questions set out later in this chapter we are considering upstream and person-centred solutions. Being person centred means being acutely aware that there are nine elephants we need to look out for: belonging, person-centred support, an interesting and active life, rapport, communication, health, family support, competent services and happiness.

The Elephant Named Do People Belong?

Belonging is much like love – it is highly subjective but hugely rewarding. We can each recognise belonging even if our own experience of it is significantly different from the experiences of others. And like love, belonging is a fundamental human attribute often denied people with IDD or autistic people: those responsible for understanding the challenging behaviour of people often fail to consider love and belonging. Why, it is almost as if those designing services do not think belonging or love matters to autistic people or those labelled with IDD. Which of course would be a ridiculous state of affairs now, would it not?

QUESTIONS ABOUT *THE ELEPHANT NAMED DO PEOPLE BELONG?*

- How can we tell if the person or child with IDD feels lonely or scared?

- How many of the same people remain in the person or child's life after ten years?

- When challenging behaviour happens, does what we do result in the person feeling more included and less alone?

- When the challenging behaviour happens, does what we do create trust?

- *What three things can you do right now to help the child or person feel less lonely?*

A person can easily be busy and at the heart of a family or service but still remain unbearably alone. To be set aside due to our unique differences is to feel bullied, angry and apart. Many people with IDD or autistic people are catastrophically alone. They may have different definitions of what belonging looks like.

Support staff and teachers regularly leave for new opportunities. Professionals often have control *over* but no involvement *in* the life of a child (O'Brien and Lovett, 1992). For many adults with IDD or autistic adults the only people they see are those paid to be there.

David Pitonyak suggests loneliness is a life-threatening issue we are often not so good at recognising. If we recognised belonging as being as important to our welfare as food we might design support very differently (Pitonyak, 2010a).

It is not simply the number of people around us that determines our belonging – a large network of people is only an opportunity network after all – but the nature of the interactions these people provide. Having choice about who supports us is as important as *how* they support us.

If the person feels alone or surrounded by people paid to be there, and if their history features broken promises and fractured friendships, we are gaining an insight into a life lacking in things we ourselves take for granted.

Could it be possible we do not ourselves show challenging behaviour not because of our ability to communicate or our skills, but in part because we are surrounded by people who love us, who are bothered about our happiness, and who cut us a break *because* we are viewed as an equal? It is salutary to compare our lives to those with IDD living in hospitals or schools or services so many miles from home. It is important to compare our lives to the lives of profoundly affected autistic individuals labelled by the apparent difficulty of others to get to know them rather than their gifts and perspectives.

EXERCISE 1

1. Around a picture of a child or person using services write the names of the people who spend time with them, or who have had some impact on their lives over the last two years.

2. How many are paid to be in the person's life?

You will probably find that for many people with IDD or many autistic people there are more people paid to be in their lives than not paid.

Reflective Questions

1. What does being paid do to relationships?

2. If this were the case for the person you love most in the world, how would you feel?

EXERCISE 2

1. Around a picture of a child or person using services, draw three concentric circles. Each circle represents a level of income.

2. In the innermost circle, write the names of the people who are paid the minimum wage (or below) to be with the person. In the next circle, write the names of people who earn 20 per cent above the minimum wage for being with or advising about the person. In the final outermost circle, write the names of those earning 50 per cent above the minimum wage for being with the person or advising others about the person.

You will probably find that the less time people spend with the family, child or adult with IDD the more they get paid. They may well know the person in the centre the least. You will also notice the further away from the person they are the more 'power' others enjoy: a psychiatrist will see the person the least, be paid significantly more than others and have more influence.

The Elephant Named Is There Regular Person-Centred Support and Planning?

There is a story of a local government commissioner in the UK having person-centred planning explained to him by a group of parents. This commissioner is rumoured to have said, 'Wait, what you're saying is we should *listen* to a person with disabilities about what is important to them, and then do it?' 'Yes,' one of the parents said. The commissioner rubbed his head: 'What the hell have we been doing for the last thirty years if not that?'

Person-centred planning and person-centred support are elegant but profound. Person-centred planning assumes all people have the ability to influence people around them. Person-centred planning describes the support required to deliver a desirable life now and in the future. Good planning is a roadmap to delivering what is important to the person. It describes what life is like now and what it might be like. In giving the good life measurable dimensions by describing it, person-centred planning provides pathways and maps to those eager to support the individual. A good person-centred plan is a promise.

There are different plans for different circumstances and different questions. If we wish to discover how better to support a person today we ask a different set of questions than if the goal is to describe a desirable future. In person-centred planning, professional voices are balanced by the voices of families, those benefiting from support, and the people who know the person well (Mount, 1998).

Both person-centred functional assessment and person-centred planning appeal to those seeking an understanding of things impacting an individual (Wagner, 2002). Where person-centred methods are artful and often look at 'the big picture' of goals and accomplishments, behavioural approaches are embedded in scientific culture, and often focus on specific elements of a life. They can balance one another (O'Neill *et al.,* 2015) and complement one another beautifully (Kincaid, 1996). Person-centred approaches tell us where we are heading, while behavioural approaches can contribute to our getting there. Good practitioners are skilled in both (Kincaid and Fox, 2002).

Person-centred planning therefore challenges the assumptions that those who are paid the most, who are furthest away from the person, and spend the least time with them, know what is best.

One critique of person-centred planning and support might run along these lines: 'You're just guessing when the person cannot tell you directly what they want.' This is almost correct but for the assumption that only if people can tell us directly can we say with certainty what their preferences are. Many humans are not very honest the whole time – perhaps you have noticed – and some tell white lies, some lie by omission and some tell whoppers so big they make the eyes water. And some simply comply with those in authority, too scared to tell us what they truly think. Therefore just being able to speak is not the same as telling a true account of what we think or want.

In person-centred planning and support we try out things the person *seems* to be suggesting through their words or behaviours, but we change what we do in the light of how they respond (Holburn and Vietze, 2002). The responses of the person shape up our new attempt at delivering what the person seems to require: 'Some people's ways of communicating leave the important people in their lives unable to hear their views about a life that would make sense,' O'Brien writes. 'These other people have little choice but to create a story with a valued and central role for the person, whose preferences remain ambiguous. Then, these people make adjustments based on the person's responses to the real settings and experiences that resulted' (O'Brien, 2002, p.412).

A person-centred plan is a jumping-off point. It creates a series of promises that people work to adhere to. Completing a plan is taking the first step in a long road to a desirable future that is often further away than we might imagine. A person-centred plan focuses commitment and energy to create the type of interactions and the type of activities that can lead to specific goals being achieved. If a person-centred plan provides details of how to teach or support better, it is likely we will see challenging behaviour reduce: there will be less friction between the individual and the places and people where and with whom they spend time.

Person-centred planning that leads to person-centred support acts as an antecedent intervention, that is a way of supporting individuals that minimises those aspects of support or teaching that predict challenging behaviour. Person-centred support is not an ideal but the job: we discover what the person needs and we deliver it by building support around the person (Sanderson *et al.* 1997). The plan describes how we support the individual.

QUESTIONS ABOUT *THE ELEPHANT NAMED IS THERE REGULAR PERSON-CENTRED SUPPORT AND PLANNING?*

- Has a person-centred plan been created?
- Does it describe a good life now and in the future?
- Does it describe how to better enable the person's learning?
- Do support plans describe ways to achieve short-term goals and long-term accomplishments that are derived from the person-centred plan?
- How are the individual's views represented in the plan?
- Do people who know the person well verify the plan?
- Does the plan improve how the person is supported, described or thought of?
- Does the plan build the capacity of the person?
- Is the person living the kind of life they prefer?
- When the challenging behaviour happens does what we do increase the choices available to the person?

The Elephant Named Is the Person Living an Interesting Life?

Person-centred planning is learning about people in order to create a good quality of life (Mount, 1998). There is little point in creating a person-centred plan if we are not able or willing to deliver the life it describes. It is easier to contribute to the creation of a good life the more able one is. This means staff must be skilled at enabling people to do things they enjoy. Many people with IDD or those profoundly impacted by autism rely on skilled and active support to bridge any gap between ability and achievement. But active support does not naturally happen: an environment providing active support has to be engineered (Mansell and Beadle-Brown, 2012). To enact the goals of person-centred planning a way of actively working to achieve them is required.

Person-centred active support is a model of organising the way we support people. It asks us to consider the benefits to our health, well-being and status of being active in our homes and communities. To achieve an active and interesting life people need to plan and be proactive in providing opportunities for the people they support to engage in meaningful activities. To do this people need to be organised and know who will do what and when, preparing in advance the different options. People must know how to communicate clearly with the people they support, knowing how the person prefers to be supported, and how to engage people in interesting activities.

The people providing the support should be able to recognise opportunities everyday life throws up: if it is lunchtime, rather than prepare things *for* people, we will prepare food *together*. By actively planning to involve people in their own lives and activities, we provide the attention people want in a way they prefer it, rather than following an incident of challenging behaviour (Felce, Jones and Lowe, 2002). There is good evidence to suggest that adopting strategies to make life interesting and more predictable can contribute to a reduction in challenging behaviour. In effect, person-centred active support improves the quality of support and results in an improvement in quality of life, so lessening challenging behaviour for many individuals.

Active support is designed to better support adults with IDD living in group homes and commensurate provision; its principal assumption is that being involved, busy and sensitively supported throughout the day, week and years is beneficial. Living an interesting life is living an ordinary life, something that far too many people receiving support might consider extraordinary, because an interesting life offers opportunities for refinement of communication skills, rapport and learning.

QUESTIONS ABOUT *THE ELEPHANT NAMED IS THE PERSON LIVING AN INTERESTING LIFE?*

- Before calling for behavioural advice, do you know if the person is living a busy, interesting and varied life of their choosing with activities and people they welcome?

- What does the person enjoy doing?

- How often do they do these things?

- Can you increase these?

- How many regular and predictable activities in the house involve the person?

- How many opportunities exist to experience new places, people and activities?

- If you are working in a service, how is your time organised? How do you know who will do what when and how?

- Every activity can involve someone in ways large and small: do people by default do things with or for others?

- Are activities meaningful to the person?

- When challenging behaviour happens, does what we do safeguard the person's chosen activities and opportunities, or does what we do reduce choice and activities?

The Elephant Named Is Rapport Encouraged?

If my day is spent with people with whom I lack rapport, no matter the activities or their professionalism, the day, frankly, drags. If I'm spending time with those I have established rapport with, time flies and I have much more fun.

Rapport is a crucial ingredient in the delivery of good support. Often it is not the programme's brilliance that changes behaviour but how we support people. Rapport, like communication, is an often-ignored attribute of a meaningful life lived within a web of relationships.

Rapport simply means we share common interests, we like one another, and we understand each other. As a result, people enjoy spending time together and cut each other a break. To communicate effectively we need to share a code, but to communicate joyfully we need rapport. If the person we are with is uninterested in us it is unlikely they will hear us or heed us.

Poor rapport is a predictor of us *not* communicating, a signal for us to *not* share ourselves. To support co-operative interactions, the ebb and flow of give and take, it is helpful to have good rapport.

Noticing something good about someone, mentioning it in passing, can sometimes begin to rebuild trust and grow rapport. Rapport is often overlooked because it is so common sense. But these days, common sense is a superpower:

'What does the person enjoy or need?' I ask.

'We don't know.'

'Go find out.'

'But he's got autism.'

'Autistic people enjoy and need things.'

'You can't say "autistic people", it's offensive.'

'And not knowing what a person prefers *isn't* offensive?'

We know we do not have to wait for planets to align or fate to intervene in order to develop rapport, because often it just happens – people click very naturally – but some relationships take time and a little work.

Rapport can take time to develop because we need to learn about each other: what the person enjoys is not always common knowledge. But if you want to invest your time in discovering the interests, preferences and personality of a person, you are likely to receive a not inconsiderable dividend: reciprocal rapport.

You can spot two people with good rapport because they pay attention to one another – they notice what the other is doing. It takes only one person with good rapport to defuse quickly an escalating situation. Investing in rapport is akin to saving into an emotional bank account (Covey, 2004): the more regularly you invest, you more credit you can call on. Perhaps this is why we speak of 'paying attention'.

How on earth do you achieve rapport with an individual showing challenging behaviour, or who has profound IDD, or is severely impacted by autism? Ephraim's work is relevant here in that the first step is to take the person seriously. Next, 'associate yourself repeatedly with a wide variety of activities, people and things the person values, then eventually your presence will become a signal that many rewarding activities and events are available with you' (Carr *et al.*, 1994, p.112).

Now it is possible you both got off on the wrong foot: in 'emotional bank account' terms, you started a little overdrawn. To help reset relationships, you might do well to avoid a battle of control and simply spend time creating a list of all the things the person enjoys. You can do this without words: each time a person turns away from an activity or person or experience gives you a clue as to preferences. (If you can't think of anything the person enjoys, perhaps there's your issue.)

You then invest time in naturally providing preferred activities and items the person values. Don't make the person earn anything – these are not rewards – simply provide preferred things naturally. Soon you may be associated not with unpleasant demands but with positive experiences. Like any investment you reap a dividend the more regularly you invest, and rapport building is not a single event but (like person-centred support) continuous. You know when rapport is developing when both you and the person seem happy to spend time with one another. It is often helpful to think about developing rapport slowly and in small bits. The last thing you want to do is swamp the person with your presence as you might end up *damaging* rapport. If the person runs for the hills when they see you, you might need to step back a little.

Some family members or support staff might well consider your time with the person as merely an indulgence: 'You're too busy having fun to be really working.' Work and fun are not incompatible and an investment takes time to mature. Soon you will be able to demonstrate to others that your time has been well spent.

FIRST QUESTIONS ABOUT *THE ELEPHANT NAMED IS RAPPORT ENCOURAGED?*

- Before calling for behavioural support, are relationships with the person secure or ruptured?

- Do you know the person's preferred items or activities?

- Are these provided abundantly and for free?

- Do you share common interests?

- How involved is the person in selecting the people who support them?

- Are these people actively working to deliver a good now and an even better tomorrow for the person?

- What does the child or adult value about those around them?

- When challenging behaviour happens, does what we do keep relationships safe and respectful?

Your time with the person may well have fewer incidents of challenging behaviour. You may well discover you both actually like hanging out together. It would be helpful to us all if we ensured we build into our busy lives time to discover more about one another and to identify shared interests. Our professional identities occasionally act as a barrier to spending time together.

Support staff may be told it is not their role to discover common ground. They may be told time at work is not theirs to invest. Support staff should not be made to think being involved in support excludes hanging out together in low-demand but enjoyable situations. Dave Hingsburger suggests that if we spend as much time *being* with someone as we spend *doing,* our understanding of one another might increase (Hingsburger, 1998). Eventually people can be encouraged to discover that the elephant in the room that is a lack of rapport is less to do with ability, more to do with attitude.

Developing rapport makes a lot of sense because having a rapport can make learning more enjoyable and quicker, but primarily because getting on with people makes life very much more enjoyable. By having good rapport you become a signal for enjoyable experiences. You are a signal that says, 'You can get things you like from me.' A benefit of investing in rapport is that the momentum you have built up can carry you through difficult times. In difficult times you can make a withdrawal from your emotional bank account by reminding the person they know you, they trust you, you will always be there for the person, but right now their behaviour is not making anyone's life easy.

SECOND QUESTIONS ABOUT *THE ELEPHANT NAMED IS RAPPORT ENCOURAGED?*

- Do we have time to simply be with someone or do we have to be doing?

- Is our role defined by the things we get done or the time we invest in relationships?

- Is the manager of the service a micro-manager or an enabler?

- Do we share our interests and skills with people or do we have to act like robots following a programme?

- Do we feel able to say, 'Hang the schedule, fancy going out for a picnic?'

- Do we know what makes the person laugh?

The Elephant Named Is Communication Someone Else's Problem?

We know communication is cited as a common barrier to understanding autistic people and people with IDD. It is often said *their* receptive communication skills are poor or how *they* express themselves makes it difficult for us to know exactly what they mean. But as the great philosopher Winnie-the-Pooh noted, perhaps it is up to us to remove the fluff from our own ears.

Less commonly cited (because who would pay to research this issue?) but equally influential on our work to understand challenging behaviour is *our* ability to communicate with one another. Our ability to organise things well is often a significant elephant in the room in many of the meetings I attend.

It is also the most highly camouflaged. It sometimes feels to be in every professional's interests to blame others for not communicating when if we were honest we ourselves fall short of the expectations we place on parents or colleagues.

In services for autistic people or people with IDD, specialist knowledge abounds. There are silos of expertise in departments of psychology, nursing, speech therapy, care management, social work, occupational therapy, psychiatry and the myriad of other professional identities we have grown over the decades only to complain there is insufficient money reaching frontline services. And whilst most often different specialists are bound together in teams, the reality is that not all teams work together to deliver seamless provision because not everyone knows how to organise teams to make them effective or efficient.

It is often valuable to chart the journey families and children with IDD or autistic people travel. Their travelogues are often descriptions of crooked maps and unexpected redirections, long delays and changing faces. The path parents describe is seldom straightforward. Unnecessary obstacles are experienced. Too often the very systems intended to support families cause anxiety and frustration.

Seeking advice from a suitably experienced or qualified professional in order to be guided toward helpful strategies makes sense, but gaining access to busy and hard-pressed specialists is easier said than done. At a meeting about how services to families should be organised the following was heard: 'We just need to make sure parents know where they fit into our provision.' Which struck many as the tail wagging the dog.

Professionals are a rationed resource but they cannot afford to be precious about being useful or available. As people exquisitely trained in specialised approaches, professionals have an obligation to pass on freely what they know to those who will make use of it. Families, support staff, autistic people and those with IDD are not grist to the professional service mill. Professionals are there to deliver a service, not squander resources and argue about how many angels are dancing on financial pins. People with IDD and autistic people do not exist to justify the jobs of professionals. Families should not be expected to leap through hoops of fire in order to gain the information or support they require or are entitled to be given.

If teams around the child or adult cannot communicate or work together, the overall service provided will be a poor one. Communication is everybody's responsibility. If communication is 'the intentional transmission of meaning in a formal code between people who share that code' (Coupe and Jolliffe, 1988, p.104), then those around the child or adult must understand one another and speak a common tongue or at least have handy translations available. We should be pulling together, not talking apart.

Professionals can easily lurch into specialist lingo because such language marks our identity and territory. Our specialism means we know things others do not. By using specialised vocabularies we effectively set ourselves apart from others. Language too often is used to emphasise our own status. While families wait for services to become coherent and relevant their lives goes on and many families succeed not *because* of but *despite* professional involvement. If supporting a child can be conceptualised as a project then professionals and services are the most valuable sub-contractors. Parents and the people we serve are actually the project managers.

QUESTIONS ABOUT *THE ELEPHANT NAMED IS COMMUNICATION SOMEONE ELSE'S PROBLEM?*

- Do professionals, services leaders and parents demonstrate good communication practice themselves?
- How is what we do promoting communication between teams and professionals?
- Are people working in partnership or at crossed purposes?
- When challenging behaviour happens, does the response of professionals help or hinder the situation?

The Elephant Named Health

Having a toothache or earache, having a urinary tract infection or a migraine will change how people respond to others. We recognise the role of pain and illness in our own behaviour; however, doing so in children or adults with IDD or autistic people is less common. We may ignore illnesses because they are less obvious than the disability we can all too readily focus upon. Checking with medical staff to investigate and treat illnesses is one of the elephants in the room we can often benefit from identifying early.

In Chapter 4, 'Behaviour is Lawful even when Awful', we introduced the idea of there being two types of antecedents: *setting events* affect the reinforcing potential of *predictors*, that in turn signal a certain *behaviour* is likely to be *reinforced* as a consequence of the behaviour. We know we need to consider carefully:

- illness and pain (e.g., constipation and reflux)

- epilepsy

- allergies

- tiredness or fatigue

- hormonal changes

- the impact of medication

- food deprivation and diet, including caffeine (Emerson and Einfeld, 2011).

because these physical issues may be acting as setting events or establishing operations to challenging behaviour.

We should consider physical wellness carefully. It is sometimes difficult to ascertain symptoms so having health professionals with knowledge of IDD is vital. For example, the chances of diagnosis of hearing loss in a person with severe or profound disabilities is small for a number of reasons, including not least the clues about the individual not hearing being misinterpreted as a sign of their cognitive processing. We know hearing loss is under-reported. People can mistakenly think misunderstandings arise due to disability not deafness.

As part of the 'management of challenging behaviour', medication is often prescribed. There is evidence of the over-reliance on psychoactive medication in people with IDD or autistic people whose behaviour challenges the system. Indeed, the Stopping Over Medication of People (with learning disability, autism or both) (STOMP) initiative by the NHS and partners has begun to have a significant impact on awareness of such issues (NHS, 2018).

The many side-effects of certain of these medications are often not fully considered. A part of any health assessment must be a medication review, especially an awareness of the side-effects, which can include general sedation, headache, depression, changes to appetite, mental confusion and thirst.

Finally, by focusing on interactions between individuals and those around them we should not ignore the presence of particular biological factors such as genetic conditions. Some conditions have been correlated with increased prevalence of certain behaviour. For example, people affected by Prader–Willi are likely to show issues associated with excessive appetite, picking of skin, and eating non-food items. A systematic examination for the potential presence of such genetic phenotypes (conditions associated with certain types of behaviour) can help inform the approach used to teach alternative behaviours.

QUESTIONS ABOUT *THE ELEPHANT NAMED HEALTH*

- Does the person have regular dental and medical checks?
- When was the person's sight and hearing last examined?
- Has medication been reviewed in the last six months?
- What alternatives to medication prescribed 'for' challenging behaviour have been considered?

The Elephant Named Supporting Families to Be Strong Partners

Families can be an incredible source of knowledge and energy. No two families are the same and it is therefore problematic to generalise 'wants' and 'needs' without immediately thinking of exceptions. Family is as families are: forget demographics and definitions. If a group of people identify as a family – regardless of number, orientation, gender, abilities – so be it. These things might not be our choice of situation but to be fair this really is not about us. Being asked to attend a family is an invitation to engage empathy as well as knowledge. The benefits of hanging out with people who know about their child cannot be over-estimated.

Research tends to suggest many families of children with disabilities seek clear information about the practical implications of disability or difference, about the type and range of services or supports available, and about best practice (Santelli *et al.*, 2002). The role of advisors is to stay focused on the immediate issues at hand whilst being aware of the vital need to support families to remain strong and coherent as they deal with often incredibly stressful situations. Richard Hastings's work on the stress of staff and families needs more attention (e.g., Hastings and Taunt, 2002) but the key point these authors make is that parental well-being impacts a child's behaviour and vice versa.

Li-Tsang and colleagues challenge the trope that having a child with disabilities or differences is inherently stressful by noting that many parents experience joy as well as stress and that special needs are different from intractable problems (Li-Tsang, Yau and Yeun, 2001). These authors focused on seeking to determine those strategies that are beneficial at fostering coping and constructive attitudes within families. They suggest children with disabilities or differences can act as contributors to family cohesion by focusing the energy of the family members. Realistic and positive expectations of the child seem to help, as does a good level of parental education, pragmatic problem-solving skills, and resilient personalities. The key finding of this small study is that parents value local support networks. Professionals or advisors have a potentially useful role in signposting such networks to families. The way the advisor or professional communicates can affect how families feel they can cope (Bromley *et al.*, 2004). It is worth remembering that parents may not be at their wits' end, only tired (Green, 2007).

A network of families is akin to a community of practice – an informal group of people sharing common interests and skills –

in that they provide emotional and practical support as well as information support. Belonging to a community of people sharing similar experiences can contribute to the well-being of families. Parent-to-parent support models offer a way of gaining support that does not rely on busy professionals. Expertise is dispersed in such parent-to-parent networks – there is no single authority.

The emotional support provided by people who have experienced similar situations is invaluable. Emotional support might include knowing one can call on an ally who has 'walked the same path' as well as being able to provide practical support. Having people available who want to share their knowledge whilst listening with an uncritical ear can really contribute to success. Being a family including a child with disabilities or differences is often exhausting *and* joyful – disabilities bring a range of additional demands, not least the requirements to bring others into the very heart of family traditions (Kincaid *et al.*, 2002).

Families are sources of expert knowledge, hard won through experience. All too often, however, we hear tales of the voices of families being silenced or ignored. It is as if the stories families tell and the knowledge they have acquired, not being certificated to university level, can be dismissed. Such approaches are self-defeating (Danforth, 2000). If we make families dependent upon professionals we disable families. When being told the news of a disability or difference parents say they prefer people who are able to speak of the practical implications as well as who encourage questions and show emotional sensitivity (Jan and Girvin, 2002). Such sensitivity should not stop once a diagnosis is made.

When advisors or professionals meet families, there appear to be some useful principles to consider adopting.

1. *Dump the gloom.* Not every family is experiencing heartache or bereavement. Plenty are, but many are too busy forging new ways of being a family or too busy 'doing family' to focus on what they do not have (Summers, Behr and Turnbull, 1989). We sometimes hear people mention the word 'suffer', in that the child 'suffers' from epilepsy or they 'suffer' from Fragile-X. Ten minutes in a room with a family, an advocate or a person

impacted by difference or disability and the person mumbling 'suffer' may have a *completely* different perspective on suffering.

2. *Be useful.* Eric Emerson noted psychologists could easily be more plumber, less Ivory Tower theoretician (Emerson *et al.*, 1998). This is sound advice for all of us contributing to understanding and responding to challenging behaviour. Families usually want partners not critics. Finding a partner who listens remains, for too many families, a remarkable event: it would be grand to witness remarkable events become commonplace.

3. *Language as code.* Active listening is an interpretive act and has been widely discussed in PBS for many years. It is most often mentioned within reactive strategies (see Chapter 8, 'Hits Happen'), implying people only listen carefully in a crisis. This is, of course, immensely daft.

   It is helpful to listen carefully *before* a crisis, as listening carefully *all the time* can *avoid* a crisis happening in the first place. To be an active listener requires us to cease being quite so literal and rather seek to understand what might be meant rather than said. Being aware of the nuances of communication and our own responsibilities in communication partnerships sets apart those who achieve and those who struggle to form good rapport with families.

   For an entertaining afternoon, actively listen in meetings. People talk a lot, and people use big words and high concepts, but too often it is a form of warfare. By actively listening it becomes clear their posturing and use of authoritative terms communicate their lack of solutions, originality or contribution to the wellness of others. The language we choose to use should not obfuscate or confuse people but illuminate understanding. (Did you see what I did there with my ironic use of 'obfuscate'?) Behaviour advisors have learned to sheath their language and speak to people in a manner the situation requires. Too often language is used to belittle parents. One too many mentions of *positive reinforcement* and you run the risk of becoming an *antecedent* for being shown the door – and more importantly, excluded from the knowledge held by family members that our expensive vocabulary has alienated.

Coventry is nice, but an inadvertent or even intentional use of technology-speak will mean you'll be visiting that particular city alone. Language can help you align with families or it can build a wall.

4. *Be honest.* Sometimes behaviour *is* awful. It's frightening and mystifying. Frankly, it can be stomach churning and disgusting. But it's good to know that behaviour is lawful.

   Your job is to keep reminding family members who might be at the raggedy edge due to sleep deprivation and sneers from neighbours that this is something they can work out and work through. The last thing to do is downplay the awfulness. Don't tell family members to just 'buck up' or cheerfully to 'work through it'. Do not tell them the attributions about their daughter hitting herself are merely 'a social construction'. You have to be honest in acknowledging that the crap does not smell like perfume. It stinks. But…working together means finding a way toward solutions.

5. *Don't be a hero. Be a host.* Who doesn't want to be a hero? A hero provides the answers (and many of us want to be thought of as useful). But as Will Rogers is said to have noted, being a hero is the shortest lived profession on earth. I *could* live alone and write pastiches of Great Russian Novels (they all die in the snow) but being in a family and being loved is far more fun than independence, at least for me. We practitioners might do well to remember it is not us up at 3am trying to implement a stimulus control strategy for a child with suddenly five arms, six legs and the ability to spit through the eye of a needle at seventeen metres.

   Listening to these tales means our analytical expertise may not be of prime importance. Heroes are fine on the cinema screen but in real life enablers and team players tend to be more welcome.

6. *Come down off the Cross, we can use the wood.* This line from Tom Waits' song 'Come on up to the House' seems sound advice – it is easy to blame ourselves when people do not listen, when our carefully crafted plans head south for a while, or when people give us short shrift for genuine efforts. Rather than bemoan, gnash teeth or condemn, get your own support. I heard a story of one person advising another to 'treat others how you would want to be treated yourself' but a *third* person pointed out that most people treat themselves terribly – always blaming themselves, never getting enough family time, working all hours, not investing in liking themselves. You are allowed to get sad, but just make sure after a little while you give it back. Work out how to avoid feeling like that in future. Cut yourself a break.

7. *Do not be reductionist, be expansionist.* In using PBS we are *allowed* (nay, expected) to think systemically. During your exploring (in other words, our assessment) of situations, do not simply focus on 'target behaviours' to reduce. Plan to increase family-enhancing behaviours and accomplishments. Plan to increase happiness and fun. Whilst the child may be the focus, family members are equally important allies in bringing about change and should be supported. Aim to nail the issues and nail the contexts, too. Never 'treat' a single behaviour. Do not manage behaviour, support positive behaviour: it is radically different.

    Love is a key feature in families and we overlook it at our peril. But love is never simple or elegant or prone to formulation. Love often features contradictions and fears. Being a parent often involves seemingly incompatible ways of thinking, such as accepting difference and wishing there was *no* difference:

    > Parents who want simultaneously to love and heal their children are old hands at finessing the fact that caring requires that we believe incompatible things at the same time. That is, parents can accept the value and importance of their child's obsessions and the beauty of their different ways of

experiencing the world around them, even as they work to free them from restrictions... (Silverman, 2012, p.235)

Taking account of how people *feel* is an important element of our work.

8. *The Right Stuff.* What we count might not count to families. What matters to families might not matter to the metrics of effectiveness our employers seek. Our role then is to support those requiring access to our experience, *and* to educate those responsible for designing provision and services because current metrics of efficient service delivery do not account for much that families might value. Families often want a good quality of support, not a fixed number of 'sessions'.

The small things a family seeks are not small things to them. The small reductions in money or support signed off by commissioners are not small things to families. Not affording someone the support they need and should in law expect means those with the least get less. Today's budgetary savings store up problems for tomorrow and the pain flows down the generations.

This is inevitable when we think services are the only answer to the needs of families. Thankfully, services are not the only source of support.

As practitioners we have a choice to be exactly what the family needs or precisely what they do not. There are many powerful examples of the positive impact of PBS on family and friendships (e.g., Fleisher, Ballard-Krishnan and Benito, 2015). But let's not be zealots. There are examples of awfulness that *claim* to be PBS (in *hospitals*, in *units*, in community work). These bear the same similarity to PBS as pornography does to love. We have to remember that values as much as science are the foundations of PBS.

> **QUESTIONS ABOUT *THE ELEPHANT NAMED SUPPORTING FAMILIES TO BE STRONG PARTNERS***
>
> • Does your advisor regularly have 'professionals only' meetings to which you are not invited?
>
> • Are families fully involved in decisions or fobbed off?
>
> • Families are advocates. Their vested interests often include the happiness of the person they love. What is the vested interest of the professional?
>
> • Professionals that are often most respected by families share similar experiences or are very good at listening more than they talk. Does the professional you know talk first or listen?
>
> • In a professional's report, do you recognise your son or daughter?

The Elephant Named You Call This Competent?

Many adults rely on the competence of others to support them to achieve a good life. But if the people who support them are indifferent, uninterested or distant, if they are unclear how values are enacted, if they are unclear about maintaining person-centred support, if the culture they work in does not learn from mistakes, it is likely conflicts will be an everyday part of life, and so challenging behaviour will grow.

Yet one of the common assumptions we encounter in Serviceland (they do things differently in Serviceland) is that supporting autistic people or children and adults with IDD is a low-skilled job. There is also an assumption that all services, all managers, all support staff are created equally, and any service will do.

Clearly, supporting children and adults is highly complex and nuanced. Management of services and the leadership of staff are likewise highly skilled roles. We often encounter assumptions about competency but competency is measured by the delivery of quality of support to staff, families and those using services, not by qualification alone. Competency is achieved through what is done, not what is said.

Punk rockers were incorrect in assuming anyone can play guitar. Most people can pick up an instrument and beat it into submission but it takes skill to play a good tune. And learning any skill takes time. It comes from practice. Not all provision is created equal and not all services are fit for purpose despite being purchased by commissioners. Good provision has to be engineered and carefully planned, it does not simply happen. The quality of provision for adults and educational options is a little like the curate's egg in that it is fine in places, fairly rotten in others.

In Serviceland today in the UK doing the right things has been replaced by talking about doing the right things. Much time is spent on websites, gathering outlying success stories to propagate the idea these are mainstream experiences, and in inclusive meetings planning things that will often never be implemented. In many ways, talking is the job.

People can be forgiven for thinking that talking about something is sufficient because talking people achieve promotion, praise and a pay rise due to talk not doing. People using services don't care about grand designs, but about having regular people who know them and support them well to achieve an interesting life. Many parents feel unable to criticise services or schools because what is offered is often the only option available. Many parents feel they are unable to make suggestions to professionals for fear they will find themselves excluded or labelled as being 'difficult'.

Good services, schools and professionals will make it clear they welcome 'difficult': having a critical friend to identify how situations might be improved is incredibly helpful. Having a family member who speaks of love and for the whole child or person can help raise the eyes of everyone in the meeting from their important reports concerning peg feeds, epilepsy medication, risk management strategies and so forth, and to the bigger picture of how these essential things contribute to enjoying life. The job of 'difficult' people is to hold power to account and ask uncomfortable questions.

'Difficult' people are often those able to recognise a too-good-to-be-true story when they hear it. They can spot an inaccurate support plan from the other side of the room. A 'difficult' family member is not someone needing to be silenced or subverted, a thorn-like problem to be soothed or removed, but someone to be recruited into the shared goal of delivering good and accountable provision. A 'difficult' support worker is not someone who questions authority for the sake of it, but who questions dubious decisions for the sake of the person they are paid to support. Heaven knows services need people to keep them on their toes as well as supporting their efforts, because too often statutory agencies examining places for minimum standards of support and care may be insufficient to ensure the well-being of people using services.

Most parents don't need perfect provision or saint-like staff, but they do need good enough people and honest services to do what they said they would do. 'Good enough' starts by accepting our errors and recruiting 'difficult' people to help us improve. Quality is a crooked map. Quality and questions go hand in hand and both are the duty of everyone.

These days many people claim knowledge of challenging behaviour, and practically everybody you meet will say they know *all* about positive behaviour support, even if they only slept through a half-day online webinar. Good PBS practitioners may not have a university-degree qualification but they do know how to lead by showing. Good PBS practitioners can spot a phoney and work out how to move them out or shape them up to be competent, because organising the delivery of a good life is too important to leave it in the hands of people unable to differentiate one end of a telescope from another.

If you visit a competent service for those whose behaviour challenges others you will see:

- people busy in activities and relationships that are meaningful for them

- consistent support that grows communication

- clear routines that are predictable to the individual being supported and their support staff

- demonstrable choices being offered, made and respected

- evidence of great rapport in interactions

- constructive, proactive and non-punishing support

- maintaining good health and well-being are a key component of support plans

- people are being taught new skills and experiencing new opportunities

- decisions blend data from assessment and lived experiences from gathering people's stories

- people using services and delivering services influence how things are achieved

- managers and senior staff regularly enact and demonstrate best practice.

These criteria were developed by the PBS Academy (2016) to help us recognise PBS in practice and as a field guide you might do a lot worse than keep these definitions in mind when visiting services that claim up is down and red is yellow.

PBS practitioners often face a common dilemma in needing to be in four places simultaneously. Knowledge is costly to acquire, expertise expensive to hire and time is money. Being in high demand to help others understand challenging behaviour and respond to it coherently is both an indictment of the lack of resources available *and* reassuring one will never be short of employment. Undertakers think the same, I am sure. But unlike undertakers, PBS practitioners often work through others. Good practitioners of PBS are practice leaders.

Practice leadership is not training, as we know it today. It is teaching by showing. It is the difference between the apprenticeship approach to learning a particular set of skills and going away to university (or doing stuff online) for two years to learn theoretical response to hypothetical behaviours. I would rather someone with years of good experience and reflective skills supports those I love most, not someone who once read a book on a related subject. PBS practitioners thus remember the very many hours of 'formal' training they will no doubt provide will not automatically result in a better quality of service. Training is insufficient but it is a helpful beginning because it shares information about what *could* work if we did it.

Blunden suggested that quality-conscious services grow culture from values. (It's not the number of teaching plans that count, but the quality of their implementation, and the fact the plans teach something the person using services values.) Blunden noted that the views and experiences of customers are the key concern, and argued that services keen on maintaining quality might well turn out to be less hierarchical, more democratic and more fluid:

> with small groups and task forces being formed around the solution of particular problems. The formal structure of the organisation would not be allowed to get in the way of achieving results. Staff would be actively encouraged to innovate and to champion new ideas. There would be recognition that not all new ideas would succeed. Failure would be tolerated and lessons learned from the experience. (Blunden, 1988, pp.109–110)

PBS practitioners, knowing the foibles of what human service systems do to humans, as well as being familiar with the rational science of our often seemingly irrational species, are uniquely skilled at *leading* change, coaching and modelling helpful approaches. PBS practitioners, being practice leaders, roll up their sleeves and get to work with what they have: they prefer not to wait for a perfect world (Blunden, 1988).

There are differences between service managers and leaders. Managers follow the path set by a leader whereas leaders do the right thing when there is no path. While managers do things right, leaders do the right thing required by the dynamic circumstances (Bennis and Nanus, 1985; Shackleton and Wale, 2000). Without practice leadership, a service bumbles through. Bumbling through is not good enough for the growth and continuance of competent provision. A competent environment can:

- identify the opportunities for the child or adult to be involved, be happy, be taken seriously

- describe solutions without making a referral for expert advice

- deliver what each child or adult needs

- keep their promises by working around barriers that will appear

- support its members to learn and value themselves as well as those around them

- be open to trying to think differently about people

- Show not only evidence of best practice but also evidence of the everyday application of values.

Thinking differently about people and behaviour is also known as reframing. In some situations it appears people around the person are focused on changing a behaviour that to others is not significant. Some people want the person to stop *all* challenging behaviour prior to them beginning to work with them to increase quality of life. They seek to oblige the individual to be quiet, docile and compliant. They will ask you to help the person fit in to their service.

Resisting people expecting you to fly in and fix the person, patch up the behaviour, stitch together the ripped apart is frankly hard, especially if you are being paid by the people doing the asking. The reality is behavioural practitioners will be asked to perform the minor miracle of amputating a challenging behaviour from the environment. The ethical thing will be to help those asking for such miracles to consider truly their own contribution to challenging behaviour.

Some people want to keep hold of the elephants while asking you to make the person being squished to simply adjust to the weighty presence of the elephants. Such views need challenging.

If you hear a person tell you repeatedly something cannot be achieved because it is impractical you can safely assume you are in the presence of a manager. If on the other hand a person listens to you and constructs with you innovative solutions to barriers, you are spending time with a leader.

Life is too short to waste it in provision that is simply not good enough. The person who decides is the individual using services, not strangers, not staff. Our duty is to help providers of services to think about the need to spot and relocate elephants in the room rather than fix the person.

If we see that challenging behaviour appears to be a reasonable response to an unreasonable person, lifestyle or environment, it is not ethical simply to agree to seek to change the challenging behaviour. This is where PBS hits its stride by challenging unsuitable environments.

People whose behaviour challenges those around them have the right to ethical and constructive support to ameliorate those behaviours in a manner that does not demonise them, demolish their confidence, infringe on their rights, or punish them for being who they are. A competent service does none of these things.

QUESTIONS ABOUT *THE ELEPHANT NAMED YOU CALL THIS COMPETENT?*

- Are there local high-quality services available to you?

- Does the service welcome difficult questions?

- Does the service evidence those characteristics set out by the PBS Academy?

- Is practice leadership seen?

- Is the service shaped around the person or is the person expected to fit in with the service?

- Do those buying the service consult in meaningful ways families and people using the service?

The Mother of All Elephants Named
The Question of Happiness

This section is longer than others because elephants tend to be so much bigger in reality than on television, even the invisible ones. If just one of the elephants in the room is not addressed there is an increased chance for unhappiness. Poor rapport, poor communication, poor health, a lack of person-centred support, poorly organised and led services, and not involving families are likely correlated to unhappiness.

You will discover that many children or adults with IDD, and autistic people relying on services, have multiple elephants in their rooms. These elephants can all too easily squeeze out happiness. Many good staff know how to support a person to fix lunch and what makes them happy.

You might rely upon my telling you I am happy. But I might not know you, I might not be wholly honest with you, I might repeat back what you've suggested. Worse still, I might be aware you hold the keys to my home and then of *course* I'll tell you I'm happy because you hold a lot of power over me. We can validate my statements by observing my behaviour: does behaviour match words?

If we support an individual with severe IDD or a profoundly impacted autistic person – sufficiently severe to result in them being unlikely to be able to clearly *tell* you – you might create a list of clear definitions of behaviours associated with happiness and see how often they occur. Imagine you discover that the frequency, duration or intensity of my 'happy' behaviours are not as high as they might be. Collecting such information is useful if it is used to change relationships and support to refocus them to deliver happiness and fun. You might then ensure more opportunities for experiencing things I enjoy. You might explore new experiences I might enjoy based on what you know I enjoy now. You always start from the individual 'is at', and build from where they are comfortable.

You might discover the things that make me happy by asking those around me. But the chances are my friends and family will know more about what makes me happy than my doctor. You might verify whether the people around me know what they are talking about by seeing if I behave as if happy when I do those things.

An alternative way of discovering what makes me happy is to run what is called a preference assessment over a few days and in different places with different people. By systematically seeing my reactions and choices when you offer them to me you might end with a useful description of the things that seem to make me happy. You might also simply let me loose amongst a host of items and see which I regularly select.

Of course, if you know that certain situations seem to make me unhappy, the support strategy might include:

- not putting me in that situation

- changing how that situation is presented or organised (make it fun, make it social, make it shorter)

- embedding that situation in things that do make me happy

- ensuring that *before* a non-preferred thing I enjoy a preferred thing

- ensuring that *after* a non-preferred thing I enjoy a preferred thing.

A little happiness can go a long way whereas a little unpleasantness can last and last. Like other elephants in the room, increasing happiness might be considered an antecedent strategy because it aims to reduce the occurrence of challenging behaviour by amending situations that are associated with it. Like rapport, good communication and having an interesting life, being happy tends to involve an increasing number of activities in a variety of places with a number of interesting and not stuffy boring people. Happiness is good practice and good science (Reid and Green, 2006). *Plan* to have a good day, do not expect it to happen by default.

As we move on in the next chapter exploring why challenging behaviour is happening, it is important to remember that if we can understand what predicts and follows challenging behaviour we can gather information to understand what predicts and follows happy behaviours. A lot of people spend a significant amount of time measuring challenging behaviour. Some people experience hours rolling around the floor, shouting, being restrained and being humiliated. All those hours planning for the worst might be better used planning for happiness and *avoiding* problems.

By focusing on challenging behaviour we are sometimes guilty of blindsiding efforts to identify and grow opportunities for happiness. Too many organisations earn a fortune from maintaining people in unhappiness.

QUESTIONS ABOUT *THE MOTHER OF ALL ELEPHANTS NAMED THE QUESTION OF HAPPINESS*

- What does it look like when the person is happy?
- What makes the person happy?
- Do you know what the predictors are for happiness?
- What are the consequences of the person being happy?

- Do you have a long, *long* list of the activities, people, places, music, games, movies, sports, types of food, types of drink, types of stories, ways of being addressed, clothing, shoes, hairstyles, toiletries that make the person truly happy?

Farewell, Elephants

This chapter asks us to look for elephants in the room that hamper a happy life. If just one of these elephants appeared in *your* room, your life would be poorer and we might see you show some significant, impactful and unusual behaviours. In response, I would hope we would not seek to medicate you, pathologise you, blame you or refer you to a treatment and assessment unit hundreds of miles from the people you know and love.

You would want us to seek to understand your behaviour in the context in which it occurs, which is not in a hospital but at home, at work, at play. Sending you five hundred miles from the places and faces you know in order to assess your behaviour at home seems at best an exercise in radical stupidity, at worse a fig leaf to cover the lack of local provision or expertise.

You would hope that as we account for your more impactful behaviours we would seek to discover what is going on in your life that influences your more unusual behaviour. We would achieve this by asking big questions about your life. We would not necessarily need to complete a person-centred functional assessment immediately. We would simply remove any elephants we discover.

At the same time they are discovering elephants in your room good explorers will make a note of the dimensions of behaviour, noting the size of its impact – how often it happens, how intensely, or for how long it lasts. Good explorers discover what leads to unhappiness and what leads to happiness. They use the same methods to chart pathways to different end points in order to design a roadmap that leads to happiness. Having removed the elephant, a good explorer can compare the size of the impact of the behaviour before and after the removal of the elephant. Challenging behaviour is a barrier to an ordinary life only if we have a critical failure of imagination, values and capacity to keep listening to what the behaviour is telling us.

When we first meet a person whose behaviour challenges those around them, the severity of their reputation may act like the sun – it may be so bright that everything else is thrown into shadow. The severe reputation of the person we wish to meet draws our attention to such a degree we fail to notice the elephants in the room. So look away from the reputation, and keep an eye out for elephants.

KEY POINTS FROM *THE ELEPHANTS IN THE ROOM: ON BEING PERSON CENTRED*

- Before calling for advice on behaviour support, it is often useful to check for elephants hiding in the room. It might be the elephants stepping on toes that are causing challenging behaviour.

- These elephants are called belonging, person-centred support, an interesting and active life, rapport, communication, health, family support, competent services and happiness.

- If you fail to address these elephants it is likely your endeavours to address challenging behaviour will not amount to much.

Keeping your Human Well-Nourished: Mary

All too often humans see what robots do not. One of the benefits of nurturing your inner human is the human's ability to creatively solve the blindingly obvious. Spend any time in Challenging Behaviour Land and you would begin to wonder, as Herb Lovett often did, just who had the so-called learning issues: the people obliged to use services or those running them.

One person – let's refer to her as Mary – enjoyed leaping on a select band of (usually attractive) male staff when she did not get what she needed. Soon Mary worked out how to generalise and maintain her behaviour in many settings. After only a little while Mary would jump on whole *groups* of people at a time. Many of the staff were not even remotely attractive by conventional standards. Mary attended a day centre that one day changed its routines after consultation with senior managers. Mary became less occupied than before and subsequently asked to go home a lot. Staff at the day centre said 'no' a good deal and expected Mary to follow the new routine that worked so well for them, not so well for Mary. The trouble with robots is they think everyone *else* should be a robot.

So Mary hit a member of staff *then* jumped on her, and people came running from all over, because in an emergency staff you thought dead for decades miraculously appear. When these people materialised Mary jumped on them too (because Mary was now *very* good at jumping on people) and the staff said, 'Hey, you can't do that! Go home! You need to learn to behave! Stop challenging us!' But Mary *was* learning how to behave: staff were teaching her *all* the time. One day I watched with frank admiration as Mary put on her coat *prior* to hitting and jumping on staff: when Mary got sent home she wanted to be good and ready. I was there working with another person, but Mary caught the eye with the same panache as a staff member's groaning caught the ear. Nobody could ignore Mary once she jumped on people, though most people ignored her when she did not jump on them.

A robot was initially consulted about all this jumping, and this particular robot decided Mary's behaviour was a result of psychosis, a condition associated with Mary's diagnosis. This supported the day centre's view that Mary was too challenging for them, *inherently* so, and that Mary should find alternative arrangements. Mary's advocate begged to disagree.

A more human investigation into what was influencing Mary's unhappiness and her jumping-on-people behaviour found not only significant changes at the day service but that:

- two people Mary knew well and lived with had recently died

- older team members had left, replaced by new and younger staff

- a new management approach to promote independence consisted of Mary being told to 'go fix yourself a drink' while they had an important meeting to talk about supporting people; Mary liked making drinks *with* people, you see, and didn't want to be wholly independent

- Mary had moved into a bedroom on her own for the first time in her life

- there was inconsistent staff interaction at the day service and in Mary's home: everyone everywhere was doing their own thing

- Mary's medication had been increased to manage 'problem behaviour'

- Mary's relationships and trust in staff was breaking down due to behaviour

- privileges were being withheld until Mary could 'behave'

- Mary had been living in a hotel for a couple of months while the house she was familiar with was being refurbished.

The home and day centre focused on Mary being the problem. They wanted to focus on behaviour and ignore the elephants in the room. Their voices were louder than the voices announcing the imminent arrival of elephants in the room. They wanted professionals to measure Mary and *solve* Mary by judicious use of data. Professionals declined – they wanted the home and day centre to do something about the elephants being fed and watered.

In the end the day centre banned Mary, and then the home told Mary she had to leave because of 'reorganisation'. They would rather make a woman homeless than remove elephants.

Mary left the day service, left her home of fifteen years and spent half a year in an assessment service where she stopped jumping on people on account of them jumping on her first. A life can spiral downward very quickly when people who should know better are pushing you hard from the top of a helter-skelter.

Many service robots expect humans using services to be nice, grateful, constrained and compliant, even if their lives are falling apart. Robots become affronted by people's behaviour. The people I work with are said to 'have' challenging behaviour because the behaviour they display is either dangerous to themselves or others, or an affront to staff. This is probably why I enjoy the work so much, and why I welcome hanging out with people who challenge, because I have a lot in common with the people who challenge.

Traditionally we might say Mary's issues were resolved when challenging behaviour reduced. Mary's challenging behaviour reduced not through medication, not through a carefully worked-out assessment and support programme but by her getting a life. People worked to fix the issues of which challenging behaviour was a symptom. Getting a life is one of the 'secrets' to resolve challenging behaviour because challenging behaviour often is a symptom of not having a life (Risley, 1996). It is a very human approach. It is also at the heart of person-centred planning and action.

Where behavioural (or any kind of) intervention can go deeply, awfully, troublingly wrong, is when people get caught up in seeing things from their own robotic point of view, not the other person's. When we think our opinion is more important than the views of others, when we do things *to* the person not *with* them, we can be fairly sure we are channelling our inner robot. The troubling thing is that robotic techniques can be used in ways so they have impact despite the human's objections.

It may not be the reinforcement programme that is reducing one behaviour by strengthening a competing behaviour. It may simply be the person on the programme is ground down and hopeless, and cannot be bothered to fight any longer. It may be that what is making the person happy is having people in their life who deliver nice experiences, not because they follow a programme robotically. It might be that a change in behaviour isn't down to the reinforcer you think.

In my experience, most change comes about not because of the carefully worked out schedule of reinforcement events (a token, a drink, a cigarette every 45 minutes, say), but by the human exchanges that happen *between* the programmatic rewards: a smile, being noticed, delivering what the person enjoys: general not specific reinforcement.

KEY POINTS FROM *KEEPING YOUR HUMAN WELL-NOURISHED: MARY*

- Challenging behaviour often means someone is experiencing a challenging life.

- Dealing with the elephants standing on a person's life can usually be relied upon to reduce challenging behaviour.

- Never underestimate the power of being bothered about someone, and doing things to make life a little easier.

Franny: How We Listen

Asking someone about how they're thinking or feeling is a big ask, especially given they may not know us. We're asking them to trust a stranger. They may be a little nervous, they may acquiesce to whatever people in power (such as professionals, such as grown-ups, such as parents) say. In Franny's situation, the people endeavouring to listen to Franny, to elicit her own thoughts and feelings, are known to Franny or have focused on first growing a positive rapport. We who ask questions are required to be trustworthy. Such trust comes not from qualification or position of authority, but through small moments of listening seriously to what the person has to tell us.

When visiting a new country, it is often best not to be loud or judgemental about the new place, but to be sensitive to local cultures. It is best to visit, not import our own prejudices. Slowly, we can discover tacit knowledge and local secrets rather than jumping in with our own bias-boots on. People are much like a foreign country in this regard, Franny especially.

Franny has agreed to talk with someone once a week at school. Miss Roberts is a learning-support assistant in a different class but Franny often seeks Miss Roberts out in the playground. Franny enjoys these conversations and says she likes having Miss Roberts to herself. They have begun to discuss how Franny feels about school ('I hate the other children') and home ('I don't know what's going to happen to me').

Here's one extract from a conversation:

Miss Roberts: 'And when you pinch yourself?'

Franny: 'I don't want to tell you.' *(Franny is staring out the window, not making eye contact. She is knocking her wrist against her chair.)*

Miss Roberts: 'That's OK. You can talk when you want to.' *(She smiles.)*

Franny: 'Some things are secret.' *(Franny looks at Miss Roberts's shoes. The wrist-knocking increases in speed.)*

Miss Roberts: 'Forever?'

Franny: 'You don't understand.' *(Franny picks the skin on her knee.)*

Miss Roberts: 'I might.'

Franny: *(Franny looks briefly at Miss R.)* 'No one understands.'

Miss Roberts spoke with Franny's class teacher about this and later the head teacher, Miss Neruda. The school staff do not feel they can share these conversations with Franny's parents right now. They have phoned the educational psychologist who often visits the school, as well as the education authority's behaviour support service.

Other children have begun to tease Franny. Not every day, but often enough to make Franny withdraw even more into herself. When Mrs Irving, the class teacher, called a meeting to remind children of the school rules (Be Kind, Be Thoughtful, Offer Help Not Blame), two children said they thought it was unfair Franny received special treatment. If *they* wanted to leave the class they would not be allowed to, whereas Franny is given ten minutes to run about. A long class discussion followed: while rules are for everyone, different children need adjustments.

While Franny is by no means the only child with separated parents, Miss Roberts has overheard children teasing Franny. Franny now spends a lot of time with grown-ups when she is at school. She still chats with Miss Roberts but seems unwilling to share too much about home. Miss Roberts has responded by less chatter, more colouring – one of Franny's favourite activities. Miss Roberts thinks it is important to remove any demands in order to help Franny feel comfortable in their sessions. The school have introduced a series of reward points for kind behaviour and good work for all children. However, at one school assembly, when Franny was given a Gold award for collecting twenty reward points, and after Miss Neruda told Franny she was a good girl, Franny shouted, 'I'm not a good girl!' and ran out of the assembly.

At her homes, Franny has told her parents she wants to shower on her own, without their help. Franny's mother Lynne thinks Franny is approaching puberty a little early and that this wish for privacy is natural. Both parents have said they have seen a reduction in self-harm but there seem to be more meltdowns. Both put this down to a combination of the changes in circumstances and hormones. Lynne's approach is to encourage Franny to go into the garden where she calms down. Lynne keeps an eye on her from the kitchen window – her partner Molly does the same but thinks they need to be a little firmer in telling Franny what is good and bad behaviour.

When at home with her father, John tells Franny to calm down in her room, a place crammed full of stuffed toys and cushions Franny chose. John sits outside her shut bedroom door while Franny shouts and rages, during which John speaks to Franny. 'I tell her she's OK. I tell her it's OK to be angry. I tell her I love her.' When Franny quietens, John speaks to her through the door. 'It must look strange – symbolic, too – to be speaking to one another through the door. We argue through the door, we do fart noises through the door, plan dinner, tell jokes through the door. When Franny's calmed down, when she's explained to me what I did wrong or what's frustrating her, *she* opens the door. I never open the door first. And I don't reprimand her. Afterwards, she usually wants a long cuddle, but she won't talk about what upset her once the door is open. Last week she put a finger over my lips as I was speaking as we hugged. I got the message.'

QUESTIONS ABOUT *FRANNY: HOW WE LISTEN*

- What do you think Miss Roberts is concerned about?
- Is it right to not share these concerns with Franny's parents?
- Is the support the school provides helping Franny learn how to cope with frustrations?
- How might you support Franny at school?
- How might you support Franny if you were Lynne or John?
- What kind of support is the school receiving?
- Who is supporting Lynne and John?

CHAPTER 6

Exploring

Understanding a Different Story

It is perfectly legitimate to focus on wholesale improvements to the quality of life, communication and well-being of an individual as the primary initial method of intervention. Doing so may well reduce challenging behaviour to such an extent the severe and negative reputation of the individual dissipates. Sometimes, despite these effective approaches, dangerous behaviour continues. This means we will all benefit from exploring challenging behaviour in a little more detail. Just be aware that your love of reducing the issues down to specific behaviours that are easy to define and measure can make you oblivious to elephants in the room.

Magic! Pick a Behaviour, Any Behaviour, but Don't Show Me the Elephant

Elephants in the room usually affect many behaviours, so dealing with the elephants has a generally beneficial effect. In the same way that there is no medication able to reduce a single behaviour – medication impacts *all* behaviour – there is no specific behaviour that will not be affected by improving the quality of life of people through the removal of elephants. There are significant side-effects with many medications and there are side-effects with improving quality of life. We might discover the child or person we support grows in confidence and is able to voice their opinions, for example. They might begin to *expect* to be taken seriously.

There are times when despite dealing with general influences on behaviour we still need to understand specific issues in more detail.

Occasionally complex situations benefit from the clarity of reducing contexts down to the simple brass tacks of specific behaviours. So how do we choose which behaviour to focus upon?

First of all, everyone involved should be part of answering these questions:

- If a particular challenging behaviour did not exist, would the person's life be healthier, have more opportunities, and result in greater happiness?

- If a particular behaviour did not happen, would those around the person be better able to support the delivery of good relationships, rapport and opportunities?

If the answer to both is 'yes' and the challenging behaviour is significantly impacting the well-being of the individual or those around them, then this might qualify as a behaviour to explore with a view to understanding it better and so grow support strategies. If a particular behaviour results in people advocating for medication or restrictive management, if a behaviour damages others or relationships, damages the individual's reputation, results in exclusion or stress, then the behaviour has the *potential* to be significantly impactful, and justifies examination. A behaviour that threatens opportunities is one that needs addressing.

> **KEY POINT FROM *MAGIC! PICK A BEHAVIOUR, ANY BEHAVIOUR BUT DON'T SHOW ME THE ELEPHANT***
>
> - A challenging behaviour that damages well-being and quality of life needs addressing.

One Potato, Two Potato, Three Potato, More? Choosing Behaviours

Some individuals show a significant number of different challenging behaviours. If one is particularly dangerous, it makes a lot of sense to seek to address that. However, it is possible that particularly dangerous behaviour is the *final* behaviour in a long chain of behaviours that grow in intensity over time. (See Chapter 8, 'Hits Happen', for more on this.)

SHARON

Sharon has a severe reputation for aggressive behaviours: she grabs the hair of people and pulls them to the floor. She also punches people. Sharon's college teacher came into the profession to inspire young people, not to be a cage fighter: can you do something to stop the aggression, please?

Observations show that nine times out of ten Sharon's aggressive behaviour is predicted by shouting and screaming, which in turn is predicted by pacing, which is accompanied by finger-pulling and Sharon asking lots of questions about who will collect her after college.

Aggression is clearly the most impactful of Sharon's behaviours. But given we know there is a chain of earlier behaviours that regularly predict aggression it makes sense to focus support on these. If we do not support Sharon early things can escalate, and a cascade of challenging behaviours can occur. When we explore for the message of challenging behaviour it is often best to explore the early behavioural 'mumbles' rather than focusing on the 'screams'. It is your call but identifying how to avoid a wrestling match seems a worthy investment.

> **KEY POINT FROM *ONE POTATO, TWO POTATO, THREE POTATO, MORE? CHOOSING BEHAVIOURS***
>
> - Sometimes a more impactful behaviour is predicted by a less impactful behaviour that is perhaps overlooked: addressing the less impactful behaviour can often avoid the more impactful behaviour.

Person-Centred Functional Assessment: What it Achieves

If we have removed elephants and challenging behaviour continues, we need to make use of a more systematic approach to help us understand what is happening.

Many people think discovering why someone shows challenging behaviour is mysterious and that those able to consistently do it well use arcane methods featuring big words, impressive certificates and are close to being esoteric wonder workers. The identification of things predicting and reinforcing behaviour has more to do with science than Delphic complexity, however. Exploring why challenging behaviour occurs compels us to become detectives.

A person-centred functional assessment breaks down challenging behaviour into a 'four-term contingency' that describes what is actually happening more often than not. Challenging behaviour does not come out of nowhere. There is always a somewhere. Challenging behaviour happens as a result of other events. A person-centred functional assessment seeks to describe patterns of behaviour asking what happens before and what happens after the challenging behaviour. A behaviour does not just continue to happen because the person fancies doing it, but because it is effective in getting or avoiding feelings, people, places and things.

A completed person-centred functional assessment describes:

- the precise behaviour being examined

  - what it looks like, how long it lasts, how intense it is, how frequent it is

- setting events

  - contexts that predict when the behaviour will or will not occur (for example, feeling unwell, having a busy morning with lots of demands)

- immediate antecedents

  - just-before contexts that predict when the behaviour is likely or not likely to occur (for example, being asked to do something)

- the consequences that keep the behaviour happening (we call this the *function*) (O'Neill *et al.* 2015).

Once a behaviour is understandable it may seem less frightening. We need to complete a person-centred functional assessment because it supports the creation of a summary statement (also known as a hypothesis statement, or best guess) describing the four bullet points above: *what* behaviour happens *when* and *why*. An example of a summary statement is set out in Table 6.1.

In this example, through completing a person-centred functional assessment, we have arrived at a useful description of the functional relationships between events, Noah's behaviours, and consequences.

Table 6.1: Noah's Contingencies

Motivators	Predictors	Behaviour	Outcomes
Being tired from a lack of sleep or being physically unwell, or missing breakfast before school means…	…when Noah's non-preferred teacher asks Noah to get ready for sports activities…	…Noah is more likely to talk back, shout or walk away…	…resulting in Noah escaping the teacher's request, and gaining approving attention from classmates

Few humans live in isolation. The behaviour of others affects us and we impact others. A good person-centred functional assessment can produce a summary statement not limited (ironically) to the person (Table 6.2). Knowing *why* the teacher responds to Noah can help us develop strategies that support both the teacher and Noah.

Table 6.2: Noah and Teacher's Contingencies

Motivators	Predictors	Behaviour	Outcomes
Being tired from a lack of sleep or being physically unwell, or missing breakfast before school means…	…when Noah's non-preferred teacher asks Noah to get ready for sports activities…	…Noah is more likely to talk back, shout or walk away…	…resulting in Noah escaping the teacher's request, and gaining approving attention from classmates
Being unsure how best to engage Noah, not wanting to spoil activities for the rest of the children means…	…when Noah talks back, shouts or walks away…	…the teacher is more likely to let Noah walk away and pass the problem on to someone else…	…so the teacher can get on with teaching children who want to learn. The teacher doesn't have to deal with Noah.

Because we have many examples of it happening, we can say with confidence Noah's behaviour seems to be maintained by both *escape* from a particular teacher's particular demand, but also by gaining approving *attention* from his friends. For Noah, being a rebel is cool – it makes him feel good about himself – so we can say there are *sensory* outcomes, too. (It is better to be cool than being seen as stupid for some children, as Terri Chiara Johnston (2014) notes). When Noah challenges, the teacher has learned to let him go because it makes life easier. Both Noah and his teacher reinforce one another's behaviour. From such simple summary statements, great support strategies grow.

In the same way that it is hard *not* to spot an elephant once you know they exist, it is similarly not difficult to spot a *probable* function (the regular outcome of the behaviour) once we know behaviour must be happening for a reason. The flowchart in Figure 6.1 outlines how we might begin to understand possible functions.

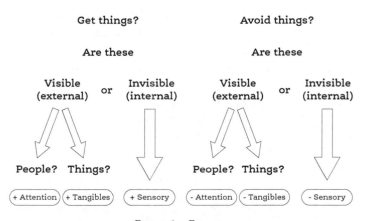

FIGURE 6.1: FLOWCHART

To arrive at a quick initial 'best guess' about what maintains behaviour we must watch what typically follows the behaviour. We will need to see the behaviour fairly frequently in different places to be sure. The more the number of examples of the behaviour we see in a variety of places, the more confident we can be about our ideas. To illustrate this, let us consider Suki.

SUKI

Suki often sits on the floor and shouts when she is prompted to do her homework by her father. It seems he only has to begin to say, 'Suki, time for homework...' and she's on the floor. Suki's mother watches for three evenings just to verify her hunches. Suki's mother sees Suki avoid homework (and Suki's father's demands) by sitting on the floor. However, Suki's mother can ask Suki to do the homework and Suki completes the task without sitting on the floor. Suki's mother suggests her husband ask Suki if she'd like a drink: 'Suki, would you like a drink?' Lo and behold, Suki sits on the floor. Suki's mother thinks this is less about homework, more about how Suki's father asks Suki to do stuff...

If Suki's mother were to use the flowchart, she might highlight it as shown in Figure 6.2.

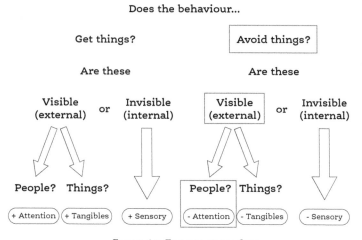

FIGURE 6.2: FLOWCHART FOR SUKI

Often we see regular patterns – functional relationships[1] – when we carefully watch what follows the behaviour. But occasionally we see different outcomes for the same behaviour.

---

1   This is not referring to a happy marriage. A functional relationship describes patterns of behaviour: a given behaviour is predicted by regular events, and outcomes are often consistent.

> **KEY POINT FROM *PERSON-CENTRED FUNCTIONAL ASSESSMENT: WHAT IT ACHIEVES***
>
> • A person-centred functional assessment describes when, where and why a specific behaviour happens.

More than One Function or More than One Behaviour?

The function of behaviour can change over time, across places, and depending on a range of other factors explored in earlier chapters. If the child or adult we are supporting has only a limited range of skills or behaviours then the chances are they will use a behaviour in multiple settings to 'communicate' different things. The more ways of behaving a person has, the more options exist for getting needs met. The fewer the skills, the fewer their options, the more likely we'll see behaviours being used for a variety of reasons.

Context may well determine function. If we see different apparent functions to the same behaviour at different times, with different people in different places, it could be we are detecting the influence of setting events (motivators). It may be rare for people to have one function for all examples of the same behaviour across places, times and people.

In the same way I feel differently when people say 'hello' to me depending on, to name just two, my relationship with the person and how I am feeling, so a good person-centred functional assessment will reflect the apparent purposes of behaviour across places, times and people. It pays careful and nuanced attention to the subtle meanings behind behaviour at different times.

This is why we need to describe carefully and *precisely* the behaviour we are interested in understanding in *specific* locations or times. Too often the definitions we are giving are actually no more than a summary label of many subtly different behaviours. Therefore, if you encounter descriptions of behaviour along the lines of 'acting out' or 'aggression', you might need to pause and redefine *precisely* what is meant. Observing closely tends to provide the best clues about the meaning or message of the challenging behaviour.

**KEY POINTS FROM *MORE THAN ONE FUNCTION
OR MORE THAN ONE BEHAVIOUR?***

- We may conclude that one behaviour has many functions (or
messages) but we need to ensure we have considered that
these different functions are not simply a product of where,
when and with whom the behaviour occurs.

- The same behaviour in different places and with different
people might have different functions, though the behaviour
looks the same.

Person-Centred Functional Assessment: How We Explore

There are a lot of strategies and techniques to establish the apparent
function for behaviour. We can ask people who know the child or
adult well to describe all the behaviours that are impactful: we can
use questionnaires or interviews, for example. Such approaches are
useful because:

- They help people feel involved in the exploration (we may be the
first person to actually ask them what *they* think is going on).

- People who know the person well can signpost us to those
times when we're likely to be able to see the actual behaviour
and when we won't.

- They can begin a dialogue where those who know the person
begin to share their tacit knowledge.

Of course, there are caveats to relying solely on third-hand accounts.
We may be unwittingly telling one another stories we believe to
be true but that are not actually the reality. During interviews and
questionnaires we may discover people have widely contradictory
views. This is useful as it suggests different responses to support
are actually making situations even more complex. Relying solely
on interviews and questionnaires to arrive at a best guess about
predictors and consequences of behaviour is not particularly safe in
terms of accuracy. But then neither is relying on records.

Historic documents can provide some fascinating clues about other people's experiences or perceptions, but relying on these is no different than relying on other third-hand accounts. I was once conducting some exploratory observations in an assessment and treatment unit when I saw an incident unfold. Once everyone was safe and calm I retreated to the office for a few minutes to make some notes about what I had seen. This is where one of the support workers found me. He had his own records to write up.[2] I knew this worker had *not* seen the antecedents to the incident: he had arrived at the end. This did not stop him completing a full and comprehensive Antecedent, Behaviour and Consequence incident record. He flicked through the other records and then wrote his report informed less by what he had observed and more by what other people had previously written.

This is why we do not rely on records to decipher behaviour in order to arrive at a summary statement. People do analyse incident records but presuming what is recorded is accurate is a hefty assumption of competence. Staff may be trained in physical restraint and risk assessment, drilled in the vital importance of recording fridge temperatures and keeping endless records about not much in particular ('Robert had a good day') but they are rarely supported to learn how to make accurate observations. Every day staff learn the price of not completing records in a timely manner but not the cost of failing to support someone in a manner that avoids a confrontation.[3] Because of such issues most good explorers use a variety of methods for discovering the meaning of behaviour depending on the circumstances.

The most pragmatic method of arriving at a summary statement is to conduct our own observations. If we wish to discover functional relationships we need to use methods that allow us to observe in real time. Observing is time consuming but basing support on unverified records or perceptions is expensive in terms of wasted effort and potential human misery, because if our 'best guess' about the function

---

2   All people with IDD living in assessment units know they cannot so much as go to the toilet without someone recording it. Is there any more comprehensive form of restraint than knowing whatever you say and do will be recorded by someone whose notes you are not permitted to correct? Won't that constrain your liberty to express yourself? The lack of privacy means each part of your soul is under scrutiny by judges not subject to the same oversight.

3   It is almost as if staff performance is measured by the records they produce not the support they provide.

of behaviour is incorrect our interventions may be ineffective. Being there to see what is happening also offers opportunities to take note of good practice that predicts the occurrence of non-challenging behaviour ('what do we do to avoid situations that predict challenging behaviour?'). People don't often record when things go well, but perhaps they should. Most services record events only when they go wrong. Careful observing means you can see both.

We can use many different recording methods. Ted Carr and colleagues suggested a simple observation card method (Carr *et al.* 1994). When an incident happens details are entered upon the observation card. The use of one card for one incident means that afterwards people might collate cards in ways that seem pertinent: by behaviour, by predictors, by consequences, for example. But their method is itself based upon a much older methodology of collecting such vital information, and I have created a simple observation form to illustrate the kind of information we would want to collect (Figure 6.3).

FIGURE 6.3: BLANK OBSERVATION FORM

Staff or parents can complete such an observation form if they have the time to do so. Often it is better for a visitor to do the recording. Any new face in a family home or service or school is likely to draw the attention of everyone, however. The longer the visitor spends in the place the more likely those living or working there will become habituated and even a little immune to their presence.

This form prompts the observer to make notes about what is likely to be important to help us discover the meaning of behaviour (see Figure 6.4). The name of the individual whose behaviour challenges, the observer's name, the date and time of the incident are entered on the observation form.[4]

In 'Contexts' we find people record what was happening around the individual before the challenging behaviour. This can include setting events we suspect may be influencing behaviour. 'People' shows who was actively involved at the time of the incident, whereas 'Predictors' tends to feature events immediately before a specific behaviour occurred. 'Outcomes' are the consequences we see or suspect have taken place following the challenging behaviour.

Name	Observer	Date 1st February
Noah	Flora	
		Time 10.20am

| Contexts | People |
| In second class session, Noah was late arriving, took a while to settle, seemed 'bored', yawning. Had been asked to read set book with class. Class was quiet. Miss T (teacher) busy marking. | Whole class. Noah was sitting next to friends. Miss T alone in class – Mr B (assistant) was in meeting. |

Predictors: Just before the behaviour, this happened...
Miss T asked class to put down their books and said 'Games up next. Go to the toilet and go get changed. Today we're doing dance.'

Behaviours: What happened?
Noah raised his eyes to heaven, something was said between him and his friends, and Noah stood up and said 'No, I want to finish the chapter'. Noah sat down and began to read.

Outcomes: What happened following the behaviours?
Miss T ignored Noah and ushered along the other children. Noah remained reading.

| Summaries: | | | |
| Contexts | Predictors | Outcomes | Verified? |

FIGURE 6.4: OBSERVATION FORM – NOAH

---

4   People often say they are concerned about recording too many incidents as their name might be associated with being a predictor of challenging behaviour. This might be possible, but it is likewise possible they are one of the few people accurately recording incidents.

If we look at the example of Flora's form, we can see key points have been circled (Figure 6.5). These are those bits of information Flora considers vitally important. To decide on what is important, Flora has examined several forms. On each, the circled issues can be found.

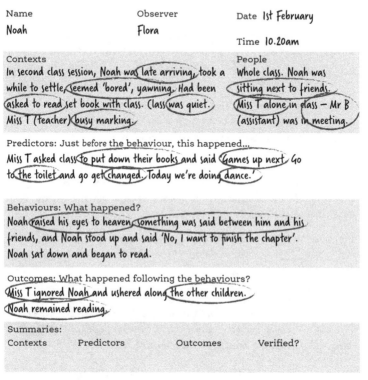

FIGURE 6.5: OBSERVATION FORM – NOAH (EXAMINED)

Flora is panning for nougats of golden information on the forms, and she has circled what she thinks is significant. The next step is to complete the bottom row. The observer (or often more helpfully a second person) summarises the key issues the form records.

In the example in Figure 6.6 we can see Flora has asked Sue to check whether her highlighted issues ring true to her. We can see that Rob also verified the findings when he observed a similar event a few days later that featured the 'story' set out on the form, namely, Noah is probably tired and busy, Noah is interrupted, Noah declines a request, Noah escapes a demand.

On the form, we succinctly tell the story of what the observation form appears to be telling us by completing the 'summaries' row.

Name	Observer	Date 1st February
Noah	Flora	Time 10.20am

Contexts

In second class session, Noah was late arriving, took a while to settle, seemed 'bored', yawning. Had been asked to read set book with class. Class was quiet. Miss T (teacher) busy marking.

People

Whole class. Noah was sitting next to friends. Miss T alone in class – Mr B (assistant) was in meeting.

Predictors: Just before the behaviour, this happened...

Miss T asked class to put down their books and said 'Games up next. Go to the toilet and go get changed. Today we're doing dance.'

Behaviours: What happened?

Noah raised his eyes to heaven, something was said between him and his friends, and Noah stood up and said 'No, I want to finish the chapter'. Noah sat down and began to read.

Outcomes: What happened following the behaviours?

Miss T ignored Noah and ushered along the other children. Noah remained reading.

Summaries:

Contexts	Predictors	Outcomes	Verified?
Noah looked tired and unengaged	Request to change and get ready for dance	After saying 'no', Noah sat down and read. Miss T ignored Noah and spoke to other children.	Sue 4/2 Rob 5/2

FIGURE 6.6: OBSERVATION FORM – NOAH (VERIFIED)

Collect enough forms and we can verify whether many people see the same story being told. You can see such form recordings are useful for beginning to collate suspicions not merely about functions (outcomes) but also about motivators and predictors.

The goal of such exploring is to have multiple forms that record events over several days or weeks. The more forms we harvest the richer the clues we reap. Once we have a good pile of forms (ideally completed by different people) we can collate them into different piles depending upon what we want to discover.

If you have recorded multiple behaviours there is a crucial first step. The type of behaviour should inform your first ordering of the forms. You sort and analyse the forms by each behaviour. We do this because distinct behaviours may have unique properties not associated with other behaviours. Self-harm, for example, might be predicted by events different than those that predict aggression.

If we want to discover common predictors, we organise the forms into piles, each of which contain different predictors. Then we count the number of common predictors. We can do the same for consequences. We might create piles for 'escape demand' or 'gaining peer attention/ laughter', for example. The more forms that show 'escape' as a consequence, the stronger our case for saying escape is the goal for Noah.

Another benefit of the form system is that, with times recorded, we can create chronological sequences of events. We might discover that Noah's more extreme behaviours are predicted by earlier minor behaviours not being resolved. We might be able to predict that Noah is more likely to become incredibly angry after three nights of poor sleep and lots of demands from teachers.

Indeed we can 'play with the information' in any way we wish. We might look for common names of people, common days or times, or contexts. The joy of the form system is the sheer flexibility of delving into easy-to-access data.

Additionally, because observation forms are physical objects we can share the work of deciphering the information on the forms with partners such as parents or support staff. Involving the people who will make use of the lessons of all our exploring might well contribute to greater understanding, and facilitate a sense that everyone can contribute to creating support strategies.

A certain way to ensure partners do not contribute their ideas for solutions is to exclude them from the exploring, and present the analysis as something only highly qualified professionals can do. If we are serious about partnership work then we enact it at each stage.

As mentioned, we should not limit the power of observing to challenging behaviour. We can conduct a person-centred functional assessment on any behaviour. During observations, Flora did just that, because Flora took the opportunities observation gives to see what good things are going on. Flora wrote up a series of forms for 'near misses' – incidents that *nearly* took place (see Figure 6.7). Flora called these 'Exception Incidents'.

Name	Observer	Date 17th February
Noah	Flora	Time 10.02am

Contexts
At start of second class session, Mr B was talking with Noah about his weekend. Class was a little loud. Miss T (teacher) was talking with other kids about the school play.

People
Whole class. Noah was sitting next to Mr B (lots of attention). Miss T on other side of room.

Predictors: Just before the behaviour, this happened...
Miss T said 'OK, class, time to get active! Go visit the toilet on the way to get changed. Today we're doing football.'

Behaviours: What happened?
Noah put his head on the desk and said 'Really?'

Outcomes: What happened following the behaviours?
Mr B laughed and said 'Yes, Noah! Really! Bet you can't score a goal against me.' Noah laughed and said 'Bet?' Mr B said 'Bet you five minutes of golden time.' Noah got changed and actually scored.

Summaries:
Contexts	Predictors	Outcomes	Verified?

FIGURE 6.7: OBSERVATION FORM – NOAH (GOOD)

Flora examined the form in just the same way she would for clues about challenging behaviour (see Figure 6.8). Only this time Flora was panning for gold concerning how to *avoid* Noah having a meltdown.

Name
Noah

Observer
Flora

Date 17th February

Time 10.02am

Contexts
At start of second class session, Mr B was talking with Noah about his weekend. Class was a little loud. Miss T (teacher) was talking with other kids about the school play.

People
Whole class. Noah was sitting next to Mr B (lots of attention). Miss T on other side of room.

Predictors: Just before the behaviour, this happened...
Miss T said 'OK, class, time to get active. Go visit the toilet on the way to get changed. Today we're doing football.'

Behaviours: What happened?
Noah put his head on the desk and said 'Really?'

Outcomes: What happened following the behaviours?
Mr B laughed and said 'Yes, Noah! Really. Bet you can't score a goal against me.' Noah laughed and said 'Bet?' Mr B said 'Bet you five minutes of golden time.' Noah got changed and actually scored.

Summaries:

Contexts	Predictors	Outcomes	Verified?

FIGURE 6.8: OBSERVATION FORM – NOAH (GOOD) (EXAMINED)

And just as before, Flora asked someone else to check her discoveries to make sure she wasn't seeing things that weren't present (see Figure 6.9).

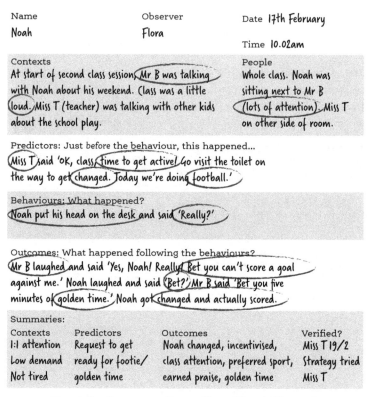

Name	Observer		Date 17th February	
Noah	Flora		Time 10.02am	

Contexts
At start of second class session, Mr B was talking with Noah about his weekend. Class was a little loud. Miss T (teacher) was talking with other kids about the school play.

People
Whole class. Noah was sitting next to Mr B (lots of attention). Miss T on other side of room.

Predictors: Just before the behaviour, this happened…
Miss T said 'OK, class, time to get active! Go visit the toilet on the way to get changed. Today we're doing football.'

Behaviours: What happened?
Noah put his head on the desk and said 'Really?'

Outcomes: What happened following the behaviours?
Mr B laughed and said 'Yes, Noah! Really! Bet you can't score a goal against me.' Noah laughed and said 'Bet?' Mr B said 'Bet you five minutes of golden time.' Noah got changed and actually scored.

Summaries:

Contexts	Predictors	Outcomes	Verified?
1:1 attention	Request to get	Noah changed, incentivised,	Miss T 19/2
Low demand	ready for footie/	class attention, preferred sport,	Strategy tried
Not tired	golden time	earned praise, golden time	Miss T

FIGURE 6.9: OBSERVATION FORM – NOAH (GOOD) (VERIFIED)

Flora did something incredibly smart at this point. Flora knew that for every person who views such observations as opportunities to improve the support they provide, there is a person who might be crushed by realising they are not as perfect as they had hoped. Flora suspected Miss T might be one of these people because Miss T was beginning to realise how she spoke might be acting as a predictor for Noah's challenging behaviour. If we want to learn what to do to avoid issues we need to learn what to do to increase competing and positive behaviour. Flora knew that what she had witnessed Mr B do worked well for Noah and Miss T might discover alternatives to her default approach by learning from Mr B. Flora thus asked Miss T to verify the form.

This gave Flora an opportunity to talk with Miss T about the information and discuss the possibility of trying out some of Mr B's strategies. Mr B's strategy ensured Noah received positive attention before a demand. Mr B's subtle use of incentives seemed to work, perhaps because choice is so important to Noah. Miss T suggested Noah should just behave like other children and Flora agreed that ideally yes, but that was not what Noah could manage right now. Miss T agreed to try Mr B's approach.

It worked. Noah complied and this verified the suggestion that it was not *always* the demand itself that triggered Noah problems but *how* it was presented. Flora, like all good explorers, never misses an opportunity to facilitate a person's learning.

For Noah the analysis of all the forms collected showed the following:

- Over four weeks, Noah showed twenty 'non-compliant' behaviours.

- Some lasted two minutes, and one lasted nearly forty-three minutes.

- Miss T asking the class to stop an activity and 'just finish up what you're doing' predicted 80 per cent of incidents.

- Seventy per cent of these were predicted by demands about getting ready for games or sport – in particular dance, golf and tennis.

- One hundred per cent of non-compliant behaviours resulted in Noah escaping Miss T's demand and continuing with reading (70%) or walking away (20%) or another preferred activity (10%).

- When Miss T reminded Noah of negative consequences to his non-compliant behaviour, Noah escalated behaviour on 90 per cent of occasions. This escalation included talking back, shouting and crying. Noah was clearly upset when facing reminders of 'punishing' consequences. Noah may be a little non-compliant but he is not stupid. Reminding Noah of penalties for non-compliance clearly does not help Noah calm down or comply in class, and it does not build trust, even if it helps Miss T feel in control.

We examined *other* 'Exception Incidents' – we recorded when Noah *did* comply or *avoided* a confrontation. We did this to gain some clues about what works best. We found:

- Noah *never* declined to get ready for football.

- When Mr B prompted Noah or agreed an incentive with him, Noah did not decline.

- When Miss T offered an incentive and gave him a signal that activities were about to change using less directive language, Noah did not decline.

- It seems apparent that having a good night's sleep meant Noah tolerated demands better than when he was tired.

In suggesting this method of exploring, a focus not merely on outcomes (consequences) but on predictor events is evident. We can detect the presence of setting events by looking at what is regularly happening some time prior to challenging behaviour. We can also look at situations that might normally predict the challenging behaviour and yet it does not happen. We can verify how possible setting events influence behaviour and outcomes by neutralising or negating these things and measuring the different levels of challenging behaviour when people do or when people do not 'adjust' setting events. (Part of your exploring is part of your solution.)

Here are some helpful questions that relate to developing a best guess about the message of the behaviour and how we might think about responding:

- Does the behaviour usually result in attention or comfort?

  - What kind?

  - Can we give this to the person without the need for challenging behaviour?

  - Can we describe a quicker and less challenging way for the person to gain attention or comfort?

  - Can the person experience a wider range of forms of attention?

- Does the behaviour often result in getting an item?

  - What is it? What are its characteristics?

  - Can we give this to the person prior to challenging behaviour?

  - Can we find a quicker and less challenging way for the person to ask for it or get it him or herself?

  - Can we discover other things the person enjoys that are similar, initially?

- Does the behaviour often result in getting away from something?

  - What is it? Is it external to the person or a feeling or pain?

  - Can we find a quicker way for the person to achieve this?

  - Can we describe multiple ways to get away from this?

  - Can we not remove it altogether or replace it?

- Is the behaviour likely to happen because it feels good to them?

  - Is the person doing this because it is the only thing available?

  - Is the person doing this because it is more meaningful to them than what is being offered?

  - Does the behaviour happen without anyone else being around?

  - Is the person busy and engaged in interesting things with interesting people?

You can see that once we have a likely function for the behaviour, we have likely support strategies bursting forth. For example, if the behaviour appears when the person is unoccupied or bored, support would provide interesting activities.

There are two final elements to consider when we begin to explore. Without addressing these two issues our careful plans to deliver a believable summary statement may go awry. The first essential is to consider the believability of our discoveries. The literature on PBS often mentions reliability, which here refers to ensuring others verify our discoveries.

We have seen when using the forms we aim to verify our findings by asking others to check out whether what we have highlighted seem the most significant clues on the form. But we can also ask if another person can verify our findings in reality. Whatever summary statement we produce needs to be verified: does the statement reflect what others see?

We might discuss our summary statements with other people involved. Does what we have discovered match their experience? But we might also ask an independent person to verify our work, perhaps through supervising our methods and practice, or by briefly seeing for themselves if our story about the behaviour matches what they themselves see. We might have a second person observe with us for some of the time. Doing this means we can compare their observations to our own. If the vast majority of the records align we can argue that our discoveries are reliable. All this is a little labour intensive but well worth it (Tincani and Lorah, 2015).

But just because our measures agree does not mean they are valid: to be valid we must measure the right thing in the right manner. For example, it is not valid to focus on measuring Noah's non-compliance behaviour when there are elephants in the room. The non-compliance might be a symptom of bigger issues. That would be akin to measuring the number of sneezes without treating the flu. The example of Franny shows this. For Franny there is a need to understand wider issues elsewhere in Franny's life rather than merely measuring running out of class. Measuring specific challenging behaviour is sometimes not the valid thing to do when the person is trying to survive a challenging lifestyle.

To verify our discoveries we:

- discuss our findings with partners: do people agree?

- keep exploring, adjusting the summary statement as we learn more.

Person-centred functional assessment is an iterative and continual process: as we create support strategies and begin the work, we can see if our summary statements are correct because of changes in behaviour. We verify as we go, checking we are still on the right track. A person-centred functional assessment is like a puppy in this way – not just for Christmas, but an ongoing commitment. The ultimate verification comes from implementing support strategies that work well for the person.

The final element to mention in this chapter is also the thing we consider *first* when invited to enter the life of a child or adult whose behaviour is considered challenging. Do we have the right permissions to be there? In the same way that each person has the right to good support, they also have the right to say 'no, thank you'. Our work simply must be subject to the laws and regulations concerning consent. Consent is a vital concern as we move toward designing support strategies. People have the right to change their minds about allowing us into their lives.

**KEY POINTS FROM *EXPLORING:*
*UNDERSTANDING A DIFFERENT STORY***

- Is the behaviour associated with certain times, places, people or activities, periods of illness, sensory environments more than others?

- Is the behaviour associated with changes in routines or unexpected events?

- Is the behaviour associated with too little or too many activities, demands, people or too much noise?

Keeping Your Human Well-Nourished: Peter

Being human includes using technology for human ends. Many people have helped me learn what it is to be human, including Gary

LaVigna and Thom Willis, who work in the US but teach all over the world. Gary and Thom's work has significantly influenced many robots to remember their human. In a book Gary co-wrote with Anne Donnellan, Nanette Negri-Shoultz and Lynette Fassbender, we are recommended to ask ourselves whether the person we are supporting has any better way to get their needs met other than through challenging behaviour. They urge us to think creatively and work in a humane manner. Having read the book as a student, I did just that. I deployed my human to such an extent that often the person I was working with utterly overlooked the need to challenge (Donnellan *et al.*, 1988).

(You have possibly noticed that many of the references are a little old. This is intentional, because there is much to learn from reading what must appear to be ancient wisdom to many people. It is salutary to realise upon whose shoulders today's researchers and practitioners stand.)

Remaining human in dehumanising systems is a challenge. Professional identities depend on robotic approaches too often. Micro-management and managerialism dominate current paradigms in established provision. No single person can bring about radical change in complex systems, but single people can band together in communities of practice to challenge ways of working and ask awkward questions, such as 'Why does Mary have to go to a day centre she hates?' or 'Why must Jane's behaviour stop before she can go out to buy the clothes she loves? Could she not simply order them online?'

Peter is eight and, reading about his life in the many files written, you would be forgiven for believing he had been referred to professional services at conception. His current issues focus on school: he dislikes maths in particular, and struggles with independent work. He has learned to escape maths by making others laugh or angry. Peter is as disruptive as a fart in a space station. Peter's teacher follows the school policy whereby any child 'acting out' has to go visit the head teacher.

This works well for Peter. He has learned to stand on his desk when confronted by a hard maths problem, because this means he is told to leave class. He also knows the chances are he'll seldom be asked to complete the maths later. (It's too painful for teachers.) Peter also quite likes being told off because it boosts his reputation as a rebel, and he likes the fact the head teacher has no idea how to respond. His teacher has learned to follow the policy because it keeps her head teacher happy, but it also means she can legitimately not teach a child who is difficult to teach and who disrupts the whole class. Both the teacher's and Peter's behaviour is being reinforced by the actions of the other. Peter has learned how to escape demands. Peter is learning, but it isn't quite the curriculum intended.

Being skilled at supporting children and adults requires us to know what the robots know without forgetting our human translation. At its best, this is what positive behaviour support aims to deliver.

A human solution for Peter *and* the teacher might include breaking down difficult maths problems into steps Peter can achieve. Knowing what Peter likes (in this case, Manchester United Football Club) might allow us to embed difficult activities in fun activities. Peter struggles with 'If Hussein has five apples and Suki has three, how do they divide their apples between a class of thirty-two children equally whilst respecting sales tax laws?' but he can tell you the goal difference of Manchester United and the differentials between each player's goal scoring: Peter is not stupid, but he does get bored by being taught in only one way *that is not relevant to him.*

Remaining human means balancing our growing understanding of the person's human story with our burgeoning knowledge of what science can bring to the party. One method to balance these related but divergent approaches is to make judicious use of compassion. Compassion is not a word often associated with challenging behaviour, but it is central to the person-centred application of PBS.

Compassion is a loaded word and has accrued many different meanings. It is pragmatic and utterly realistic to apply compassion to our understanding of and response to challenging behaviour, and it is beneficial to deploy compassion in supporting parents and direct support staff. Compassion means we recognise ourselves in others: if we have good reasons to do what we do perhaps, compassion suggests, others do, too.

In supporting children or adults with compassion we mitigate the use of harmful responses to challenging behaviour and close the apparent gulf between those with a label of IDD and those without (Vanier, 2001).

Compassion works towards growing an understanding between people but it doesn't brook hallucination or delusion: compassion is grounded, practical and everyday, it is the utter opposite of weakness. Compassion is as old as the hills and threads its way through secular, scientific and spiritual paradigms of human experience. Compassion for others has little to do with paternalism or pity, but a lot to do with sharing a common understanding of shared experiences. Compassion is taking people seriously, treating them respectfully because they are equal to ourselves: compassion means acting constructively to alleviate suffering. Compassion means using the most effective person-centred approaches available in a manner the person values.

Compassion has measurable outcomes, including increasing the development of innovative and creative solutions, psychological safety, learning, loyalty, trust, respect, motivation, retaining talented support, communication and commitment (Worline and Dutton, 2017). Being compassionate is a pragmatic and ethical attribute practice leaders can foster. Compassion *is* collaboration. Being compassionate allows us to use technology in a way that does not dehumanise others and avoids turning ourselves into robotic pastiches of people.

Robots sometimes lack compassion and they tend not to recognise suffering as a result; robots only recognise results. Robots put themselves ahead of colleagues and others and they fail to see humans as interdependent and interconnected beings. To robots, humans are things that do stuff: to robots, humans are behaving machines. To humans, humans are behaving machines but also feeling and doing and being and meaning and identity and loving machines. Humans assume a tired parent is doing the best they can, but to robots a tired parent is someone failing to deliver their idea of an ideal performance.

The effect of robots on humans is they make us feel unemployed, unworthy and unheard. Robots frustrate the hell out of humans.

A robot finds it hard to earn trust because the metrics it uses to value humans do not count human issues: a robot may know its stuff but you might not want to marry one. It is hard for a robot to tune in to nuanced but vital human concerns. When encountering a robotic response it is the compassionate path to challenge it.

It is said compassion supports our journey to understand that all humans belong to one family, but we all have family members that are tougher to get on with than others. Compassion, then, is not for the faint hearted, but for the very strong.

KEY POINTS FROM *KEEPING YOUR HUMAN WELL-NOURISHED: PETER*

- It is often helpful to use the interests and fascinations of people to frame learning and relationships.
- Compassion can help us see ourselves in others.
- Compassion is not for the faint hearted, but the strong.

Franny: A Better Understanding

The educational psychologist who works with the school has now visited to meet Franny: the report will take around two months to be sent through. The education authority's behaviour support service (BSS) has also visited and broadly endorsed what the school are currently doing: allowing Franny to leave class when she needs to, increasing the sessions with Miss Roberts to twice a week, and adjusting the school-wide reward point system. Franny can now earn more points than her peers from doing good work, returning to class within ten minutes of leaving it, and for helping Miss Roberts and Franny's classmates. The paediatrician and psychologist employed by Franny's family are happy to contribute their understanding of Franny, though so far they've not been asked for any information.

The BSS completed observations over two days. Though the presence of another adult in the class and playground was obvious, the children became used to the visitor quickly. He tried to make himself as unobtrusive as possible, but his notebook was always open and he did a lot of writing. It was obvious he was writing about *them*, the children told one another. After the first break, it was clear he was really watching Franny. This seemed, Mrs Irving said, to affect Franny. She seemed to perform – her voice became louder, her behaviour more pronounced. Being observed seemed to help Franny cope with academic tasks and negative comments from classmates. 'It was almost as if she didn't want to let herself down in front of a stranger,' Mrs Roberts said.

During the two days of observations there were two meltdowns. One happened during a science class and the other during maths. *Both* featured number work. *Both* featured Franny sitting in a different place than her usual table. *Both* featured group work. The observer noted that in *both* sessions the group to which she was allocated marginalised Franny. Franny attempted once or twice to contribute to the group, and each time was ignored. During the maths session Franny raised her hand but the support assistant did not see her. After a minute with her hand in the air, Franny shouted, slapped her own forehead, and ran out of class. During the science session the support assistant working with Franny had to leave to support another child: Franny swore before running out of class.

Often, it is difficult to see the wood for the trees. This is why it is often helpful to have a fresh and informed pair of eyes take a look at what is all too familiar to you. If you were working with Franny you might have become habituated to such events, and simply put it down to 'Franny being Franny'. A person with a new perspective would see common themes emerge: there *appear* to be predictors to Franny's behaviour, which are not about how Franny is feeling. It's what is going on around Franny that seems important.

Both incidents resulted in Franny running for ten minutes before coming back to class. (Franny has a watch and can tell the time. During the maths session the observer suspected he saw Franny glance at her watch *before* the meltdown.) Franny was not asked to apologise and by the time she had returned the activities had finished, so she was supported by the assistants to help clean up the room – a task Franny enjoys because, 'I do it with staff.'

At home, John noticed some bleeding on Franny's sheets as they were changing her bed together. 'Did you punch teddy and give him a nose bleed? He doesn't deserve that!' John joked with Franny, but

Franny didn't think this was funny. 'I wouldn't punch teddy!' she shouted. John has learned the best way to defuse a situation is simply to listen and take Franny seriously. 'You're right. I am sorry. You love teddy. Thanks for helping me understand.' Franny seemed a little anxious, John said, before Franny said quietly, 'If you love them you don't hurt people.'

John said later that afternoon he apologised for hurting Franny's feelings when he and her mother split up. 'I said we both loved Franny, only not each other. That's when Franny told me she still hurt herself sometimes. She used things to scratch herself...only not where anyone would see it.'

'What if you stop loving me, too?' Franny asked her father. John tried to say he promised to love Franny forever, but Franny said, 'That's what you promised Mum.'

John's parents paid for a psychologist to visit Franny. Mary has experience of working with children with emotional and behavioural issues, as well as with high-functioning autistic children. Mary quickly established a rapport with Franny.

Mary is from New Zealand and the two got to know each other while Franny tried to learn the accent. Mary used these social exchanges to develop a rapport with Franny. While the discussions were ongoing, Mary made some recommendations about John and Franny spending more time together, talking whilst doing ordinary day-to-day activities, and helping Franny learn it is OK to express herself through sport and art *and* conversation. Mary's conversations with Franny are focusing on growing up, and practising ways of thinking about and coping with frustrations: 'We're working on ways for Franny to like Franny, too, and to build on her love of running.'

In terms of the potential injuries arising from self-harm – both physical and otherwise – Mary is creating a list with Franny of other ways of 'harming' herself that are not so impactful but serve the same purpose, whilst at the same time opening up other ways of showing feelings. Mary is showing Franny how using ice-cubes on her skin, twanging elastic bands on her wrists, screaming, dancing wildly to music, and writing on her body using red ink – *all* are alternatives to harming herself. Franny said she sometimes turns the shower to cold – it takes her breath away. Franny said sometimes that 'pushes bad thoughts' away.

Mary thinks Franny hurts herself because doing so makes her feel she has some control, it helps her express her emotions ('Maybe Franny feels responsible for some of the hurt in this family') and it makes Franny forget for a while all the other things going on in her life. 'It is an escape, a way of feeling real, and a language,' Mary said. 'My job is to support Franny to try to find a range of languages to express herself.' Mary respects the fact that Franny only likes herself a little bit – Mary doesn't correct Franny or tell her how she should feel. Mary told John, 'This is a marathon, not a sprint. There are no easy answers, only time and learning.'

This work has taken place at John's: Franny is adamant she doesn't want her mother or Molly to know, despite John suggesting Franny's mother *needs* to know. When Franny said, 'I don't *like* Molly. Mummy wouldn't understand. It's secret,' he agreed to not tell Lynne of the work. He is very uneasy about this. Lynne has noticed a slight reduction in meltdowns at her house and has not spoken of finding any evidence of self-harm.

QUESTIONS ABOUT *FRANNY: A BETTER UNDERSTANDING*

School:

- What do the observations suggest predict a meltdown/ running out?
- What are the immediate and ultimate consequences of Franny's meltdown/running-out behaviour?

Home:

- Why do you think Franny hurts herself?
- Do you think Mary should be thinking of other interventions?

CHAPTER 7

Being There and Doing More

Support Strategies

This chapter discusses how we might organise support strategies, how we derive them from summary statements, and some details concerning support strategies themselves. The principle this chapter follows is that one behaviour will need multiple strategies that come together as a whole in a mosaic of support. A little like a jigsaw, we need to assemble all the pieces to achieve a good picture of a sound life. One piece will not provide us with a perspective on the big picture.

A Mosaic of Support

Before focusing on specific strategies it is helpful to set out how elements fit together. Doing this helps us keep sight of the bigger picture and supports our efforts to keep quality of life as the ultimate accomplishment of support.

Quality of Life Enhancements

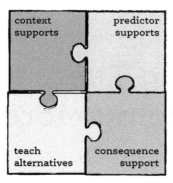

FIGURE 7.1: MOSAIC

There are several ways of organising support strategies (see O'Neill *et al.*, 2015; De Pry *et al.*, 2015; LaVigna and Willis, 2005) but each features strategies organised into a cohesive support framework that addresses all the elements contributing to challenging behaviour. Typically these include:

- strategies to increase skills or competing behaviours (proactive strategies)

- strategies to amend or avoid predictors (proactive strategies)

- strategies to neutralise setting events (or motivators) (proactive strategies)

- strategies to keep people safe if challenging behaviours occur (reactive strategies).

Whichever method is used, strategies to enhance quality of life should be central to endeavours. The purpose of each part of the mosaic is set out.

A mosaic sets out how individual elements contribute to meeting the needs and preferences of the individual. A mosaic does not aim to merely 'manage' challenging behaviour reactively – following an incident – but does include proactive or pre-emptive strategies. As can be seen in the illustrations in Figures 7.1 and 7.2, components in the mosaic match each element of the summary statement. Support strategies should neutralise setting events or motivators, amend predictors, teach alternative behaviours, and alter how people respond to challenging behaviour. Table 7.1 illustrates in a different fashion how the outcome of a person-centred functional assessment, as set out in a summary statement, links to support strategies.

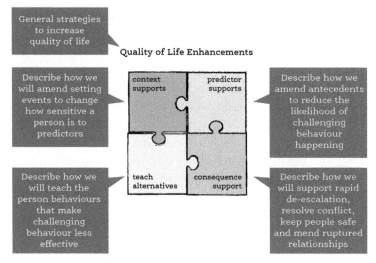

FIGURE 7.2: MOSAIC WITH DEFINITIONS

Table 7.1: Contingencies and Strategies

Four-term contingency	Antecedents (before the behaviour)		Behaviour	Consequences
	Setting events: 'motivators'	Predictors	The action	Outcomes
Translation	Things that affect the 'power' of the predictor	The signal that behaviour may be reinforced	What the person does	What follows
Strategies	Things that can neutralise or weaken setting events and increase choice	Change the messages the predictors give: amend to predict alternatives	Teach alternative behaviours that compete with the challenging behaviour	Reinforce alternative behaviours; reduce harm of challenging behaviour

Before considering examples of strategies supporting people with IDD or autistic people whose behaviour challenges others, let us examine if this approach can support others just as well by meeting an everyday grouch who seems particularly challenging to those who know him.

Making an Example of Tony: Support Strategies from Summary Statements

Here's Tony's issue: being woken unexpectedly may result in challenging behaviour. In such circumstances incoherent shouting and vigorous waving of arms (like a man unable to escape drowning in duvet) might be seen. This has a significant impact on how Tony is viewed and how Tony feels. It might benefit Tony to learn other ways of waking up. To support Tony's learning alternative behaviours, people will need strategies to deal with different elements maintaining his behaviour as set out in a summary statement (Table 7.2). Now, because the arm waving and shouting *only* happen in concert, we consider them not distinct, but part of a single event.

Table 7.2: Tony Summary Statement

Summary statement: Tony's early morning shouting and waving			
Motivators	Predictors	Behaviour	Outcomes
When Tony is tired from a lack of quality sleep or is feeling 'unwell'...	...and when Tony is suddenly woken up ('Have you seen the time? You're late!')...	...Tony is more likely to dramatically wave his arms, condemn the universe and shout...	Tony's arm waving and shouting makes people go away. Tony is then late for work, and hungry because he ran out of time for breakfast, and significantly grumpy the whole rest of the day. He feels a little ashamed, too.

Shouting and waving arms results in the demand disappearing: behaviour is maintained by escape. Given the above summary statement people agree to support Tony not to need to wave his arms so dramatically or shout quite so much, because that is harming his relationships and the well-being of just about everyone. See Table 7.3 for how we structure the mosaic of support.

Table 7.3: Tony Contingency and Strategy

	Antecedents (before the behaviour)		Behaviour	Consequences
	Setting events: 'motivators'	Predictors	The action	Outcomes
Tony's summary statement	When Tony has not slept well	When he is suddenly woken	Tony will shout and wave his arms	Tony escapes getting up
Strategies	Things that can neutralise or weaken setting events and increase choice	Change the messages the predictors give: amend to predict alternatives	Teach alternative behaviours that compete with the challenging behaviour	Reinforce alternative behaviours; reduce harm of behaviour

People identify which alternative or competing behaviours meet the same needs: an alarm clock with a snooze button. See Table 7.4 for the strategies to support Tony to learn other ways of having his needs met.

Table 7.4: Tony's Morning Support Mosaic

For Tony's morning arm waving and shouting, we have promised to undertake the following			
Context support	Predictor support	Teach alternatives	Consequence support
Find alternatives that reduce wine consumption to avoid Tony feeling 'unwell'.	If you need to talk, don't tell, ask Tony to wake.	Teach Tony to use the snooze button.	If Tony waves arms and shouts, show him the snooze button (don't speak your prompt, show it).
Have an evening routine ensuring Tony settles earlier.	Buy an alarm clock with a snooze button. An alarm clock doesn't become offended as easily as a human.	Teach Tony the joyful benefits of consuming alternative beverages the night before.	Have the smell of fresh coffee (Lavazza Rossa) and breakfast no. 2 ooze from the kitchen.

Context support	Predictor support	Teach alternatives	Consequence support
Might one contribution to Tony not sleeping well be reflux? Visit doctor to check out health apnoea at the same time. A diet might make him feel healthier. So might more exercise.	Gradual waking usually involves tea and toast (breakfast no. 1), but has been known to include a low-demand conversation about the forthcoming day. Tony often has strange dreams, so asking him about his dreams might he good.	Teach Tony alternatives to shouting through showing him the benefits of not shouting: give space and time to Tony when he uses the snooze.	Snooze available on pressing snooze button.
If Tony is drinking in the evenings, the chances are he'll be up in the night to use the toilet, which won't help his sleep pattern. Can we find alternatives to fluid? Is Tony not drinking enough during the day?		Let Tony see the benefits of getting up: preferred breakfast, appreciation from others, avoiding being late, his responsibilities to others.	

Tony is involved in the strategy design. The people most impacted by the behaviour do not write support strategies alone. Knowing Tony means knowing alternative abilities Tony has that can be shaped or built upon. There is no punishment or contrived reinforcement because the reinforcer for pressing the snooze button is the snooze, not praise. The other important aspect is that Tony has the physical and psychological abilities to perform the competing behaviour. If I can wave my arms and shout, I can reach out and press a button, and I could simply say, 'No, no thanks.'

The mosaic sets out strategies to avoid or amend contexts that make Tony sensitive to certain predictors, to learn alternatives to the challenging behaviour, and that stipulate responses should it occur.

During our exploring we discovered that if Tony has enough sleep and doesn't feel 'unwell', being woken up does *not* result in shouting or arm waving; instead Tony gets up to make everyone in the house breakfast (because Tony enjoys being helpful to those he loves).

If Tony's support strategy only stipulates what people do following the challenging behaviour (reactive strategies), Tony won't learn anything that he hasn't already learned. Additionally those supporting Tony, upon seeing no progress in his behaviour, might be tempted to use more and more aversive strategies to get him out of bed, such as throwing a bucket of water, or using electric prods. By knowing the motivators and predictors for the behaviour we together design support strategies to neutralise these, teach alternatives and help Tony not need to challenge. Each *element* of the mosaic of support contributes to resolving it. And no electric prods are required. Ever. Under *no* circumstances.

Good support strategies offer choices between an ideal performance (not shouting or waving, but getting up – usually this is the ideal of people other than Tony) and competing options that result in the same outcome as the challenging behaviour (snoozing – Tony's personal preference). Both choices are better than challenging behaviour in terms of cost, heartache and effort.

Making an Example of Tony: Competing or Alternative Behaviours

The key issue is that Tony is not obliged to stop avoiding getting out of bed – snoozes are a human right – but the support strategies do give him an alternative to shouting and arm waving, namely using an alarm clock with a snooze button. Mastering a snooze button results in the *same* outcome. Pressing the snooze button takes less effort than waving and shouting and so it is a competing, alternative behaviour. The outcome of the competing behaviour is the same as the challenging behaviour. It is what is called *functionally equivalent.*

People may well find it easier to learn alternatives to the challenging behaviour if:

- it is quicker to do, easier and takes less effort than the challenging behaviour

- it achieves the same outcome as the challenging behaviour

- it has a more immediate effect in getting that outcome.

For Tony, learning about the joy of snooze buttons is a thing worth learning. It is more immediate in achieving escape and thus sleep, it takes less effort, plus it allows Tony to slowly wake up his rational self. It is also easier for Tony's wife. Win–win solutions are more common than we think. Functional equivalence of alternative behaviours is a helpful aid to win–win.

In the exercise shown in Table 7.5, try to think of two alternative or competing behaviours that are quicker and easier than the challenging behaviour described and that achieve the same outcomes.

Table 7.5: Alternative Behaviour Exercise

Find functionally equivalent competing behaviours for...*			
Behaviour	Function	Alternative 1	Alternative 2
Shouting	Gets attention		
Shouting	Escapes demands		
Hitting others	Gets a toy		
Biting others	It feels good to bite		
Picking and digging your own arm	It feels good to hurt myself – it makes me feel real		
Sitting down in the road	Escapes shopping/gets a drink		

*Some possible alternatives are listed in Table 9.2.

You can see from this simple exercise that good practitioners of PBS often find behaviour interesting in terms of what it looks like, but what they really talk about at conferences, parties and support meetings, is function. Knowing what the behaviour achieves or avoids is the ultimate requirement to develop informed alternatives and support strategies. Knowing the function is so compelling that to an extent the appearance of the behaviour is not very significant at all beyond ease of measurement. PBS practitioners focus on understanding the purpose of behaviour, not its look. Function over form is a good maxim.

Making an Example of Tony: Quality of Life Issues

But of course, these support strategies are themselves quite limited, even though far more comprehensive than a reactive strategy alone. This is because strategies to support change around challenging behaviour do not consider the whole person or life. They are still focused on challenging behaviour, and challenging behaviour may be impactful but it is not the whole story of the person. Often challenging behaviour tells us the person is unhappy, unwell or unheard.

This is why in our mosaic plan we include general quality of life enhancements. During our exploring we might wonder at bigger-picture, almost elephantine issues. We do this because behaviour does not occur in isolation. One thing leads to another in a cascade of contingencies leading all the way back to the womb.

In Tony's example our exploring told people a good deal about when challenging behaviour happened and when it did not. Thus we arrived at the support strategies above. But we also discovered quality-of-life issues that seem to be meaningful:

- Tony is working long hours without much recognition (he feels).

- Tony enjoys wine because he says it helps him relax (he used to meditate, now he medicates with Rioja).

- Tony is starting early and working until late just to keep up with work demands: recently (say the last year) it feels to Tony that all he does is work.

How might we address these things impacting upon his quality of life? We might explore ways to make work more palatable so it does not interfere with family time. We might find alternatives to wine that can help Tony relax. And we might look at ways Tony can himself exercise some control and agency over the work demands. These strategies might involve learning ways to manage his time better, having realistic expectations, and learning to say 'no' to unrealistic demands (see Table 7.6 for some likely useful strategies). We cannot assume a good quality of life follows hard work: it will need to be planned for. We can add to Tony's support mosaic strategies to improve his quality of life.

Table 7.6: Tony's Quality-of-Life Strategies

Improving Tony's quality of life:

1. Wherever possible, Tony will move from working until a task is complete, to working until his contracted hours are complete. Tony will monitor his hours.

2. Tony will not work weekends: these are for family and friends.

3. Tony likes to work so work will be redefined not just as the duties of his employment, but things he loves (writing, family activities and learning a new skill each month).

4. Tony will explore other ways of relaxing. He might wish to rediscover meditation. He promises to go swimming with everyone.

5. Tony will ask for more regular supervision from people he admires at work, people whose experience and manner of working aligns with Tony's idea of an ideal way of working and being.

For Tony's morning arm waving and shouting we have promised to undertake the following			
Context support	Predictor support	Teach alternatives	Consequence support
Find alternatives that reduce wine consumption to avoid Tony feeling 'unwell'.	If you need to talk, don't tell, ask Tony to wake.	Teach Tony to use the snooze button.	If Tony waves arms and shouts, show him the snooze button (don't speak your prompt, show it).
Etc.	Etc.	Etc.	Etc.

For Tony, what we took at first sight as evidence of him being simply a grumpy old man who seems allergic to early mornings, transpires to be a little more complex. Problems waking up suggest wider quality-of-life deficits. Besides, sudden awakenings are only a problem when other events happen. The support strategies help us avoid or amend these other events, but they also stipulate alternative or competing behaviours Tony can learn, which are more effective than the challenging behaviour. The mosaic also teaches us how to support

Tony when challenging behaviour happens. Crucially, the mosaic highlights the need to address wider and more nuanced issues that are impacting on Tony's quality of life and thus his behaviour. Mosaic strategies tell us *how* to better support Tony to get out of bed, and longer term quality-of-life strategies give Tony a *reason* to get out of bed.

Let us consider whether this mosaic approach works in other situations by revisiting an old friend.

A Mosaic of Support for Franny

Those around Franny have concentrated on two of the most impactful issues. At school, Franny leaving class is significantly disruptive to Franny's education and for the staff and class. At home, Franny's family have agreed to seek to understand skin picking, as this is the most concerning for both of Franny's parents, though Franny herself feels this is not so important. Whilst we have robust information concerning her leaving class – we have verified the observation cards – we are less confident of our understanding of the issues that predict self-injury because we lack such detailed and verified records.

This does not mean we should not employ a mosaic model to understand where and how to inform support, but it does mean we have to be sensitive to what we do not know with any certainty. Concerning self-harm, we can speak of best guesses, little more. Let's then begin with classroom issues, given we are more confident with the information we have discovered in our exploring (Table 7.7).

Table 7.7: Franny's Leaving Class Summary Statement

Summary Statement: Franny's Leaving Class			
Motivators	Predictors	Behaviour	Outcomes
Not clear. Suspicion home situation makes Franny feel the need for more control and choice, less sure of herself (and perhaps less confident).	When a hard task is presented, or when she is teased, or when she feels unsupported…	…Franny will walk out of class.	…Franny escapes the task, accesses physical activity, expresses control, buys herself 'thinking' and 'feeling' time.

The summary statement tells us the message Franny's behaviour conveys: *I don't know how to deal with these demands.* The goal of any support will be to enable Franny to learn how to deal with these demands, and deal with them without necessarily needing to leave the class.

You'll notice the *context* strategies (below, Table 7.8) assume a difficult evening and night predicts a difficult day at school. Communication between parents and school is crucial to inform how the teachers support Franny, and the kind of tasks they offer. A difficult evening may inform how they set the level of expectations for Franny. No child benefits from a life lacking demands and challenges but how those demands are presented is amended based upon Franny's likely tolerance.

Table 7.8: Franny's Classroom Mosaic of Support

Support Strategies: Franny's Leaving Class			
Context support	Predictor support	Teach alternatives	Consequence support
Speak to who brings Franny to school about the previous evening and morning; if Franny has had a difficult time she may be tired and less tolerant of academic tasks or comments from peers.	When Franny is less tolerant of peers or demands, ensure requests are embedded in other activities, or broken down into more manageable steps. Ensure more support is available.	Franny is learning progressive relaxation during her 1:1. Remind her to practise between class tasks. Modelling is helpful.	If noting Franny is struggling (it looks like Franny is frowning; she may tap the pencil on the desk), re-present task in easier form and broken down into easier steps. Offer reassurance.
Ensure Franny is sitting with preferred classmates; ensure Franny has time with her support before a challenging task is presented.	Ensure Franny is encouraged to contribute to class discussions: give Franny responsibilities in the class.	Remind Franny she can ask for support.	Enable Franny to leave class for ten minutes. In time Franny may be encouraged to leave class for nine minutes, then eight, on a slowly reducing schedule.

Context support	Predictor support	Teach alternatives	Consequence support
Ask Franny to share how she's feeling prior to class, during break, and in 1:1 session. Give Franny opportunity to suggest solutions and how to respond to her feelings: safe space, other activities, art, running, helping teachers.	Give Franny choices about which 'harder' academic activity she can do, and in what order. Franny seems to do well with harder tasks if they are sandwiched between easier tasks.	Give Franny two options: to leave class and run for ten minutes, or to try her relaxation strategy. Reward points and thanks can be gained for either choice.	If the task is still available on her return, support Franny to complete it. If the task is finished, support Franny in a different activity. Thank Franny for returning, acknowledge this is hard for Franny because it is hard.
Feelings: Franny has designed 'mood' cards ('a bit upset', 'tired', 'worried', 'just fine', 'angry') and can show these to her support when she doesn't want to talk.	Benchmark: ask Franny to share her work every step of the task to ensure she is on the right track. Teachers prompt the correct response to small steps. This avoids failing.	Remind Franny she can leave immediately, or delay leaving for ten seconds (Franny counts to ten). Reward points and thanks can be gained.	Thank Franny for choosing competing behaviours, for coping, for 'hanging on' in class. Never miss an opportunity to quietly acknowledge Franny's contributions.
Franny loves recording her feelings on a spreadsheet and producing a graph to help her monitor how the week is going. This provides targets she sets herself.			Ensure Franny earns her reward points. Ensure Franny adds these to her reward record.

The school can arrange time for Franny to sit with those she likes because demands embedded within or following enjoyable social exchanges often reduce the chances of Franny not coping. Years of experience have taught many people offering advice that one upset can cascade into another. A series of events can escalate into a terrible day and an awful week. All too often these events lead to horrible reputations and lost years. Being sensitive to how yesterday imposes itself on today's feelings and anxieties means cutting someone a break *now* can avoid a cascade of crises *tomorrow.*

Context supports also include work around emotions. For some children or adults with IDD, naming a feeling is a first step in recognising them and knowing what to do about them. Here the school is working with Franny to help her know her own body and her own emotions: this is what anger feels like, this is what my body does, and these are the things I can do with anger: I can shout, go run, draw or speak. The message for Franny is that being angry is OK. Franny has a *lot* to be angry about. Learning the benefits of sharing how Franny is feeling with others is the not-so-hidden message of the first step taken toward expressing that anger in a less harmful manner. It is natural for those Franny shares with to offer solutions or ideas, but it is important for Franny to identify her own solutions.

Context supports also feature a self-monitoring strategy. Franny enjoys numbers and collecting data. She keeps a note of how she's feeling in a notebook and enjoys putting these into a spreadsheet and producing graphs. Once a week Franny and her support spend time talking about the meaning behind such an exploration. Franny has even decided to set her own goal: to feel happy more than angry. To achieve this, Franny has made a list of people, places and things that she can employ to increase her happiness. Franny's work on her own agency is impressive: knowing she has a choice about how she feels and can do things about it, is remarkable.

The *context supports* link to *predictor supports.* In this column people have listed the strategies agreed with Franny that can amend predictors of running out of class. These include selecting tasks based on Franny's recent past. Franny is also encouraged to contribute in class and to have some responsibilities. Often, choice is a dirty word in schools because they are obliged to follow a set curriculum in a certain order. But robots do not police Franny's school and staff are very skilled at tailoring the curriculum to individual children. Giving Franny a choice between harder and easier tasks has resulted in something strange happening. Franny, more often than not, selects the harder task provided it is broken down into easier-to-achieve steps. The staff have also discovered offering Franny an easy task before a hard task and then following this with a fun, easy task results in less anxiety. They have also discovered that if Franny shares her work with her support or peers at each step, any small errors can be corrected.

Until the world is made perfect, learning to cope or deal with unfairness is a crucial skill to acquire. This often involves two things – the ability to keep calm, and the ability to voice concerns about unfairness. For Franny, learning to relax (through progressive relaxation – see below) is enormously conducive to all manner of situations. Being able to talk about her frustrations will contribute to her ability to cope. This calming is often modelled by her support. Franny mirrors their breathing and body postures. Staff are, in effect, giving Franny a script of what to do to stay calm when they communicate to her their own feelings and actions. This sharing with other people is profound because it shows the benefit of trusting others. Franny is also offered a choice when she wants to leave: she can get up and go, or try to count-to-ten (a small delay in escape). Additional reward points and thanks can be earned by counting to ten. Crucially, these 'count-to-ten' moments can be discussed as examples of Franny taking control over her feelings. These strategies offer alternatives to running out of class.

Consequence supports set out how to respond to early warning signs as well as when she actually leaves class. They also show how to reinforce competing behaviours. It is important to remember that running out of class was encouraged to avoid a more serious meltdown in class (Franny would bang her head and scream). The school is keen to move Franny on from relying on the class-escape strategy to a whole new range of skills.

This illustrates that mosaics are not written and forgotten. Strategies grow and change as the person does. Mosaics are dynamic and great fun to be part of. The goal is not simply to avoid Franny hitting her head in class, but to accomplish a range of skills Franny can build on throughout her life. The mosaic is a good first step to the achievement of bigger things. The support mosaic is a foundation for growth for staff and for Franny.

In terms of skin picking there is much that is not known (Table 7.9). The summary statement is less robust because there were only a handful of incidents of skin picking recorded. We cannot verify the cards collected and so we are less sure of our summary statement.

Table 7.9: Franny's Skin Picking Summary Statement

Summary Statement: Franny's Skin Picking			
Motivators	Predictors	Behaviour	Outcomes
Uncertain home situations, fragile relationships, Franny insecure, puberty?	Unclear... When alone in her room at her mother or father's...	...Franny picks her skin	Control over her body, her feelings? Autonomy? Expression of feelings? Feels good to Franny?

The conceptual model we are using to organise support strategies suggests that even though we may not have identified or verified influences on skin picking, they exist. So we can use the mosaic to help us organise tentative strategies that are aimed at generally, if not specifically, addressing wider issues in Franny's life. We will examine these support strategies for Franny's skin picking in more detail after this particular chapter, but a strategy mosaic is set out below (Table 7.10). You will notice how the school work on feelings and talking overlap with the strategies for skin picking.

Table 7.10: Franny's Skin Picking Mosaic of Support

Franny's Skin Picking			
Context support	Predictor support	Teach alternatives	Consequence support
Talk and share honestly about family relationships.	Talk and share honestly about family relationships.	Talk and share.	Do not tell Franny off for picking her skin.
Reassurance through spending time together.	Nightlight.	Writing about how Franny thinks of herself: self-affirmation.	Help Franny clear up if she asks.

Context support	Predictor support	Teach alternatives	Consequence support
Mary (therapy).	Evening routines that involve parents: Franny is not sent to be on her own.	Elastic bands, ice-cubes, showers, dancing, screaming, writing on her skin.	Ensure Franny has alternative items available to those she uses to harm herself.
Opportunities for art and sport.	Landing light kept on so Franny doesn't fear leaving her bedroom to find her parents.	Running club?	Ensure Franny has clean items to pick at her skin.
Opportunities to discuss puberty.		Self-monitoring: graphing skin picking and feeling like doing it but choosing not to.	Provide Franny with reassurance and unconditional love.

We use a mosaic to organise support strategies because one intervention will not provide support to address all of the influences on behaviour. In the same way that behaviour is often complex in terms of why it occurs, support strategies are often nuanced and multi-faceted.

KEY POINT FROM *A MOSAIC OF SUPPORT*

- A mosaic comprises small support strategies that when working together create a picture of comprehensive support.

Implementing Support Mosaics

We need to ensure support strategies fit with what is happening in real life. They must be fit for purpose at home, at work and in the places the person enjoys spending time. They should fit within natural routines as far as possible (Hieneman and Dunlap, 2015). The chances are that families and support staff have been doing their best given the demands they experience and they will need support to learn different approaches, new ways of working and perhaps vitally, new ways of thinking about the individual. Supporting parents and staff to talk about their feelings, attitudes and fears is just as important a part of implementing support mosaics as learning how to perform the strategies.

Any support strategy has to be discussed and considered by all those who have been involved in creating the summary statement, and who will be implementing (or making real) the strategies. The strategies must be fit for purpose in that they are workable and fully understood by those who will be enacting them.

It is often helpful to set short-term goals or benchmarks as these tell us whether the plan is on track. Plans must change if circumstances demand it, but the longer-term goal of the accomplishment of a good quality of life is non-negotiable. We can change the route to that accomplishment, and the form that accomplishment takes may alter also.

The path from paper to doing is often a crooked one, but having a plan is a helpful beginning. It is often useful to begin with a conversation about possible strategies and then negotiate which are most doable. Once agreed, implementation is the next issue. What is needed to make the strategies a success? The following can increase the chances of support strategies being implemented:

- Practice: use role-play to confirm strategies work.

- Support: what skills do people following the strategies need?

- People: who do people call on if things do not work out?

- Benchmarks: how are successes recorded and communicated? Do we have a roadmap setting out goals and when each element of the mosaic is to begin?

- Signs of success: what does success look like?

- Signs of going awry: how will strategies be modified in the light of experience?

- Being accountable: clearly identifying who will do what by when is crucial.

Good support strategies ensure the people implementing them are well supported and guided. Coaching through practice leadership helps.

KEY POINTS FROM *IMPLEMENTING SUPPORT MOSAICS*

- Have those who know the person best been involved in deciding which strategies are best suited to contribute to an increased quality of life?

- Has the person been involved in the process? How, and to what extent?

- Have strategies been practised and fine-tuned?

Some Specific Strategies

A cursory reading of books and articles on challenging behaviour will furnish a casual reader with thousands of intervention suggestions. Each one must be taken under advisement however and guidance from an experienced and qualified advisor is required. There are no strategy supermarkets offering off-the-shelf solutions. Each type of strategy is informed by the findings of a person-centred functional assessment and the quality of life aspirations of the individual. Each strategy must be individualised to the person's unique situation and preferences.

Broad strategies should aim to neutralise, amend or avoid motivators and predictors of challenging behaviour, and teach competing behaviours. The fundamental principle of supporting behaviour change is to encourage and reinforce and grow what you want whilst seeking to downplay what you do not. The following strategies may be suitable in certain circumstances.

General Strategies Amending Motivators and Predictors to Challenging Behaviour
Interactions

Drawing up an interaction profile is a useful approach to help spread information about the best way to support people. Gather a group of people who work with the individual very well and create a list of 'golden rules' they have discovered that if followed more often than not ensure the person enjoys the day. It may be the person prefers certain routines, or enjoys particular ways of being addressed or asked questions.

Typically an interaction profile describes what methods of interactions are responded to best, how activities can be presented, and what it looks like when the person is enjoying themselves or not. It can list the range of activities the person enjoys and for how long. It can also show how to grow rapport. The rationale here is simple: if we can make interactions less aversive we can avoid conflict.

Communication Passport

Much like an interaction profile, a communication passport sets out clearly what methods of communication are most effective in different situations. Passports grow as skills are acquired or new knowledge gained and so will need to be regularly reviewed to avoid becoming static.

A canny reader will understand that these first two strategies aim to change how *we* interact and communicate with the individual. Good behavioural support changes what *we* do in order to encourage competing behaviours. In effect, communication passports and interaction profiles give us a way to get off the person's case and get on their side.

Embedding

If our summary statement suggests we ourselves are predictors of challenging behaviour we will have to change what we do in order to change the signal we have become. The interaction profile and communication passport contribute to good support and might avoid us becoming predictors for difficulties, but many of our interactions may have already taught the person to expect us to make demands they do not enjoy.

We can reset expectations by making zero demands. This means we focus on more social and less demanding interactions. We might craft an association with fun, or quiet, or music, *any* neutral activity not associated with hard work. It will take time and lots of opportunities for the person to stop expecting us to place a demand. Hingsburger warns that in our efforts to support the individual to keep busy we might inadvertently cause them distress. Our presence may cause a person anxiety. If this is the case then focusing on delivering good experiences is the first step to resetting a relationship. Thereafter we can slowly introduce demands by embedding them in more social interactions (Hingsburger, 1998).

Embedding simply means placing demands in positive contexts. Embedding is a particularly useful strategy for activities that are considered essential for the well-being of the person yet the person finds aversive (Carr *et al.*, 1994).

One young person I worked with hated physiotherapy and she abhorred hydrotherapy, so staff stopped doing these for a few days. Instead she listened to her favourite music whilst learning yoga in a low-demand and fun manner (that happened to resemble physiotherapy in terms of outcomes). We also went swimming (which she loved), which ended up, strangely, resembling the outcomes of hydrotherapy. There is *always* more than one way to achieve a goal.

Making a House a Home

There are endless things you can do to make the fit between a person and the places they live and work smoother and by so doing avoid or amend conflicts. Such context and predictor-changing approaches amend potential problems. These include identifying elephants and relocating the troublesome beasts, and they can include helping people know how best to support people by providing them with information concerning communication and interactions. We can make *how* we interact less demand-focused and more rapport-focused. Such deep enrichments of activities and relationships will likely see a reduction in challenging behaviour *because you are delivering what people need.*

Below is a list of possible modifications to how we support people that may reduce conflicts within the environment, all of which may contribute to improving quality of life:

- Changing how people are supported: 'interactions and fun'.

- Changing the expectations: 'is this too easy or too hard?'

- Changing the time: 'is the activity or interaction too long or too short?'

- Changing how communication is organised: 'speaking the same language'.

- Changing what people do with their time: 'active support'.

- Improving rapport: 'staff as signals for good times'.

- Ensuring the person belongs: 'relationships and networks not just paid staff'.

- Ensuring we do not set, or that we amend, events that lead to sensitivity to certain predictors of challenging behaviour: 'avoiding wars by avoiding triggers'. Such strategies are known as *antecedent interventions*.

- Ensuring the physical space suits the person: '*my* home'.

- Ensuring the physical space is interesting: 'I would choose to live here'.

- Ensuring there are things to do and that days, weeks and years are predictable: 'I am looking forward to…'

- Ensuring noise, space, light and heat are all suitable for the person.

- Ensuring access to tangible items such as food and drink and activities.

- Ensuring the person gets what they need as part of everyday support. If a person challenges to gain attention, give attention at other times. This antecedent intervention weakens the functional relationship between specific behaviours and specific consequences, thus reducing the person's need to rely on that behaviour.

Remember, individual strategies tell us how to achieve person-centred support, and person-centred support delivers quality of life.

Competing Behaviours
Learning to Wait

We sometimes want things yesterday though there exist persistent rumours good things come to those who wait. (But why take the risk, right?) Learning to tolerate waiting – the interval between asking and getting – is a useful life skill. (*Especially* in others – for ourselves, not so much.) So how do we help someone learn to wait?

Put simply, we can fill time. Before your drink, how about we go to the kitchen to choose and make one? Before your cigarette, let us get this cleaning done. Before your monthly salary, how about you work?

Not all delays are person-centred or take account of the individual's current tolerance of delay. If a person seems currently unable to wait five minutes for a drink, asking them to wait thirty minutes is probably not going to work out too well. If the same person is asked to help fix the drink first and that activity takes two minutes, the chances are the person may tolerate such a delay *because something is happening while they wait* and, further, *the thing they want follows*. Needless to say, the activity should be taken as an opportunity to support the person to learn how to fix a drink, perhaps, as well as time to be together and grow rapport.

A formula exists for calculating how long the person waits. If on average the person can wait ten minutes for an item, then seek to deliver the item in half that time. It is challenging to sit patiently twiddling thumbs because it makes time feel as if it is dragging on forever. Knowing what my average tolerance for waiting means, we can ensure I do not approach that limit. Once I have grown accustomed to asking and receiving after a short break, then you might slowly increase my waiting period by filling the waiting time with good things I enjoy. From five minutes, to five minutes twenty seconds, and if I can tolerate that, then increase to five minutes forty seconds, and so on, but gradually, and always checking in with me that this is working. It is easier to wait if our waiting is filled with preferred activities or discussions or styles of support. It is essential I have something to help me bide my time.

Notwithstanding any of the above, keep an eye out for elephants: why expect someone to wait to be rescued from anxiety or potential harm? Is waiting the abuse of power and control in disguise? At times it is important to be responded to immediately. Certain setting events can contribute to individuals being more tolerant of delays at one time than another and being asked to wait for thirty minutes in order to have a conversation because I am feeling insecure and unheard will not help me feel I belong. I may not want to chat about anything in particular, only whether I matter.

There are times we do not have to speak. The language of doing suffices. The story of Harry in Chapter 9 illustrates one example of this. We did not ask or tell Harry to take a drink between mouthfuls, we simply showed him a glass of water he happily took.

New Learning Strategies

To learn a new skill it often helps to possess some rudimentary version of it beforehand. For example, if you want to help teach me a sign that I would welcome a break from an activity, I should be able to move arms or hands or fingers. Additionally, it helps considerably if the new skill is interesting to me and is taught in a positive fashion. Fun and rapport count for a lot. More fundamentally, the new skills should benefit me. If you know the person well and can interpret small behaviours such as an eye point or facial expression as having meaning, you can shape up those by reinforcing them regularly. If someone looks at a drink and you give them a drink, you are learning and teaching one another.

It is incredibly helpful to create a list of all the things, activities, conditions and people that the person generally finds rewarding. You might then start by adding these to any teaching plan, but consider the following:

- Is the outcome a natural reinforcer or contrived?

  - The natural reinforcer for making a drink is to drink the drink (the drink-making behaviour is utterly not dependent on praise: 'Great drink making, Tony' does not have any impact on me apart from annoying me whilst I am trying to enjoy my drink. Stop talking, let me drink!)

- A contrived reinforcer would be to provide an additional outcome to the drink making, such as a reward token. (I know, odd, is it not?)

- Natural reinforcers are the ideal choice because they do not involve the mediation of other people who might forget to reinforce. In the final analysis behaviours that are naturally or inherently reinforcing will continue over time. Contrived reinforcement may be essential early on, but fading it and letting natural reinforcement do its work is the ideal situation. For example, communication behaviours will be learned and maintained over time if the reinforcer is what the communication naturally results in. The goal of communication is not to be told I am communicating well but to get or avoid the thing communication concerns.

• Is the reinforcer freely available or a human right?

- There are ethical issues with withholding a reinforcing item from someone who is used to having them. Do not make people earn what is rightfully theirs.

- Be aware if you select an item that is freely available the person may be satiated and therefore the item will not be as effective a reinforcer as when the person is not satiated.

- Make use of a variety of different reinforcers, and mix and match.

• Is there enough reinforcement in their lives?

- This question is significant for our hunt for elephants. Rather than identify specific reinforcers for new behaviours, perhaps we should spend as much time delivering reinforcement non-contingently – in other words, just enrich the lives of people without making them earn things that should by rights be theirs (Hingsburger, 1998).

The most effective approach to teaching is for you to be a *huge* generalised reinforcer. Be a sign for fun, engagement, treats and entertainment. Teaching should be fun not toil, and it should aim to enhance life. Skills must be relevant and immediately of use. (There is not a day goes by without every single person on the planet thanking their lucky stars for all that trigonometry they learned in school because it is so often used in everyday life.)

We may think it is a pretty nifty skill to tie shoelaces, but slip-ons mean people get outside into the sunshine quicker. Ask whether the skill you want to teach is meaningful to the individual. Does the new skill increase the person's ability to be taken seriously or achieve what they want to achieve, without relying on you?

When using a contrived reinforcer to grow a new skill, vary that reinforcer. It is easy to become bored and satiated with one reinforcer, and so it stops being very effective because it loses its power. For example, if you imagine your favourite snack being used by an unscrupulous person to reinforce a particular behaviour, it will not be so long before the very sight of that snack turns your stomach. Reinforcers when over-used can become sheer punishment. Too much praise, too much chocolate, too many smiley face stickers, and *whoosh!* I will not respond so well.

Keeping Perspective: Accomplishment, Long-Term Goals and Hope

Challenging behaviour is an impactful and significant but small part of a person's story, and it is often a symptom of the quality of that story. No matter how carefully written and enacted a support mosaic is, if it does not consider the goals, ambitions, hopes and preferences of a person receiving support it is incomplete. Support strategies for challenging behaviour should fit within broader strategies to achieve longer-term ambitions. When we concentrate our focus on immediate responses to challenging behaviour the price paid is the loss of vision.

As we clutch technical competency to ourselves and brandish certifications, we would do well to recall that in PBS values are at the heart of all the work we undertake. Our efforts to understand and respond to challenging behaviour are meant to improve the lives of the person and those around them (Carr *et al.*, 2002). Quality of life is not an afterthought but the job. Intervention that fails to consider the bigger picture is merely an example of *sticky plaster therapy*. If despite our work the individual lives without hope or love or people who are bothered about them, then perhaps we are focusing on an important but incomplete work, only part of the picture, not an accomplishment.

A person-centred plan is one method of engineering the steps towards the destination. This is why many people who work using PBS methods are at pains to point out that accompanying good behaviour support should be person-centred in nature (O'Neill *et al.*, 2015). Too often, support strategies focus on the reduction in a behaviour with quality of life kicked into the long grass, where it is hoped it will be picked up by someone else. A good life does not simply happen: it has to be planned and worked for (Gilbert, 1978). Person-centred planning can describe goals and also tell us how to engineer pathways to deliver those goals. Family experiences of PBS show the approach can contribute to improving quality of life, provided:

- there is a focus on critical behaviours interfering with quality of life

- there is effort to change places as well as people

- work is undertaken toward enhancing relationships

- everyone learns together (Fleisher, Ballard-Krishnan and Benito, 2015).

Building the Stable or Bolting the Door?

All of the above are what we term proactive strategies in that they are designed to avoid or reduce issues in advance of them. Proactive strategies build the stable. Reactive strategies set out what people should do following challenging behaviour. Reactive strategies should be about encouraging the horse to come back to the stable, not an exercise in bolting the door after the horse has gone.

Some of the most effective, non-aversive, exciting and person-centred approaches that have been developed over the last forty years have focused on proactive and antecedent approaches, and yet in practice it remains depressingly common to encounter only reactive strategies. There are various reasons for this.

First, research and best practice have yet to permeate all training and professional enclaves and so older 'management' rather than 'support' models predominate in dark corners. Second, despite best practice guidelines and policy advocating for proactive rather than reactive strategies, quality standards are often interpreted to justify the continued use of reactive approaches (the 'what if they hurt themselves or me?' arguments) at the expense of proactive approaches (and thus ironically they propagate harm). Third, many individuals and providers of training make a good living out of emphasising the risks of challenging behaviour, its supposed pathological origins and the need to use restraints in order to control and contain people viewed as fundamentally different from others – it is in some people's interests to keep people in purgatory. Fourth, there is a misunderstanding that power and control is threatened by adopting proactive and non-controlling strategies – for some people restraining others is a job they love. And finally, reactive strategies bring about a *temporary* reduction is challenging behaviour and so act as what we call a negative reinforcer. A negative reinforcer sounds an odd thing. If as a result of giving or adding something following a behaviour that behaviour happens in the future, we have a positive reinforcer. A negative reinforcer is the opposite: if as a result of removing something following a behaviour that behaviour happens in the future, we have a negative reinforcer. Following challenging behaviour, if the person is restrained or medicated, challenging behaviour may temporarily cease, if only for a little while.

This last point is insidious and dangerous. Reactive strategies offer temporary relief, not a long-term solution, but that temporary relief is sufficient to teach me to do again whatever it was that caused the temporary cessation of challenging behaviour, no matter how unhelpful it is to crafting a long-term solution. *Especially* if I am not aware of proactive alternatives set out in this and earlier chapters, my using reactive strategies will strengthen. Common reactive strategies have included:

- being restrained (physically or psychologically held)
- being medicated (being given medication to calm me)

- being threatened (future loss of rights, activities, food, or drink)

- being put into time-out (removed from the people, situations and things I love)

- having things taken away (preferred items withheld until I 'behave')

- being over-corrected (for example, if I a made a mess, I am made to clear up not only the mess I made but the whole room)

- having rights suspended.

Even momentary relief from challenging behaviour is powerfully rewarding. If an aversive experience (and remember, challenging behaviour is aversive) is temporarily removed, however that removal is achieved, that approach will be used again and again, as long as it temporarily removes the aversive challenging behaviour. We can thus argue that people who inflict harm and aversive strategies on others may not be simply bad people but addicts who know no alternative to what they do.

It turns out behavioural science teaches us even arseholes have mitigating circumstances.

KEY POINTS FROM *BEING THERE AND DOING MORE: SUPPORT STRATEGIES*

- A mosaic of strategies amends or avoids contexts and predictors of challenging behaviour.

- A mosaic of strategies includes alternative behaviour to encourage and teach.

- A mosaic of strategies does not ignore the need for advice about keeping safe when behaviour is happening, but emphasises a focus on proactive rather than reactive support.

Keeping Your Human Well-Nourished: Fred

Fred asks staff about what's happening. A lot. It can get tiresome for staff. But there are no visual schedules, no way of Fred knowing what's happening, and staff don't want to tell Fred about what few plans there are in case Fred 'becomes obsessed'. The other day a senior support worker on a long shift became fed up with Fred asking if he could go out in the bus the next day, and she said, 'You know what we always say, Fred: "Wait and see what tomorrow brings."' Fred looked at the senior support worker and said, 'But tomorrow never comes'.

A more human approach would surely be to provide Fred with visual information about predictable routines so Fred can see for himself what is happening. A human might recognise Fred isn't necessarily asking about what's happening: Fred might just be asking for company. Fred might be seeking out people to hang out with using the only way he has of asking. Perhaps Fred doesn't even *care* about what's happening next: perhaps he's trying to simply instigate a conversation.

KEY POINTS FROM *KEEPING YOUR HUMAN WELL-NOURISHED: FRED*

- Set up situations so people are not so reliant on you.

- Active listening suggests when someone asks you about what is happening, they may be seeking reassurance as much as information.

Franny: Being There and Doing More

Following the advice of the educational psychologist and that of the behaviour support service, the school has modified its work to support Franny. Because it was suspected that Franny struggled with more demanding number work and group work, the school has modified how they teach and what they expect. If staff suspect a task might be difficult for any child, they do the following:

- They make sure complex tasks are broken down into easier steps for everyone in class. Each successful step earns a reward point.

- They prime Franny by giving practice tasks.

- They make sure every pupil group in class can expect support from the teacher or assistant. They make sure each child and group knows asking for help is rewarded by gaining attention or advice (doing so earns a point): a child raises a hand if they need help from staff.

- Children can earn extra points for solving problems on their own and helping other children. This gives children a chance to explain their solutions to their peers.

- Reward points still can earn certificates in assembly, but if the child wishes, these certificates can be traded in for 'Free Time' on a Friday afternoon. At these times children can choose their own activities, lasting up to twenty minutes. The points are visible on a chart – each child can see how they're doing. There is always a chance to earn more points throughout the week. No points are ever deducted. One moment of poor behaviour does not undo a week of rewards.

- Mrs Irving introduced the idea that children can give their points to other children. This earns them an automatic two minutes of Free Time. If the class as a whole earns a certain number of reward points in a four-week period, additional privileges are given and a Class Celebration Snack Time organised.

For Franny, the school ensures she has some choice in terms of the peers she sits with. They have introduced traffic light cards so she can show an amber coloured card if she's feeling upset, a red card if she's angry, and a green card if she's fine (in reality, Franny does not use the green card – she just gets on with the lesson). At the end of each day, Franny has a five-minute review and she uses the cards to tell Miss Roberts how she felt during each lesson. There's always a moment for Franny to speak about what she did well – though Franny finds this difficult. ('I'm not a big head!')

Miss Roberts and Mrs Irving have taught Franny about graphing: how to show the number of good days she's had each week, or the number of times Franny diverted herself from melting down. Franny is interested in graphing real things that matter to her. Miss Neruda wrote a letter to Franny telling her how much Franny had taught her. The school has done a lot of work to try to find pupils who are more sympathetic to Franny and who can act as buddies to Franny in class and during breaks.

During one class, despite all the strategies, Franny had a meltdown. As she opened the door to leave the classroom Franny saw it was raining hard. This made her stop. Mrs Irving suggested Franny might want to go to the sports hall instead. But there was another class due in the sports hall in five minutes. Could Franny run round for five minutes instead of ten? Mrs Irving would be terribly grateful if she could. Five minutes later Franny returned to class. 'That's pretty impressive,' Mrs Irving said on Franny's return. Thus it was discovered there was nothing sacrosanct about ten minutes of running, and that this could be negotiated and even reduced.

The key strategies for supporting Franny at school are:

- easing the fit between Franny and her peers (making school a nicer place)

- making it easier to ask for help (gaining attention *before* a meltdown)

- breaking down complex tasks into easier chunks (making tasks less aversive)

- sharing her emotions, building friendships (improving quality of life)

- making it clear what can be earned through good work and kind behaviour (having clear expectations)

- reducing the amount of time Franny ran (the beginning of learning to cope).

At school Franny feels a little happier. Not everyone likes her, but then Franny doesn't like everyone. The number of meltdowns has reduced. The reward points help, as does breaking down complicated tasks, but the primary achievement is Franny beginning to feel good about herself. All these programme adjustments are only a means to teach Franny more profound lessons.

At home, Lynne and John's relationship is strained. Lynne found out about the involvement of the psychologist through Molly questioning Franny about why she wore elastic bands. Franny and Molly ended up arguing and Franny feels Lynne took Molly's side.

Molly thinks Franny is being 'manipulative' while Lynne thinks if John had been honest with her the whole argument would never have happened. The end result is that Lynne learned about the strategies recommended by the psychologist and asked to meet Mary. The strategies are now being used in both homes: spending more time together, talking whilst doing day-to-day activities, and helping Franny learn it is OK to express herself through sport, art and conversation. Ice-cubes, art and elastic bands help, and Lynne and Franny have learned to dance together with loud music. And if Franny enjoys running, why not *learn* to run? This may seem a natural skill, but the right technique can take you further. There's probably, Mary suggested, a metaphor just screaming to come out right here.

The key strategy at Franny's homes seems to be giving Franny the space to feel able to express herself and alternatives that compete to some degree with self-harming behaviour. Franny now feels she is taken more seriously and is being listened to.

Mary's work has taught Franny that no parent is perfect and children need to speak to them as if they simply don't remember their own childhoods.

Franny has a range of ways of expressing herself. One of these includes pinching herself, because despite everything, sometimes hurting helps. Franny now monitors and records her own behaviour – hurting herself, using alternatives, and meltdowns. She sometimes shares these with her parents but most of the time it is sufficient for Franny to look at the numbers and make a graph herself. She can see she is self-harming less, and the meltdowns are a little less frequent. Franny has also started to graph the times she *feels* like hurting herself but doesn't. The number of mornings revealing bruising, red marks or blood is diminishing ('I just wish the curve of the graph was quicker,' John says).

Life is hard and life is unfair. Despite our best efforts, there are times when things cascade, and old behaviour emerges because it is tried, tested and learned. Franny will always have the ability to experience meltdowns, and she will always know how and why she might hurt herself.

When Franny does self-harm – rarely now, no more than once or twice a month – what you do not see is anyone panicking and thinking all the progress has been lost, all the work has been for nought. Whilst the artificiality of the strategies has faded into things the family do every day as a matter of course, Franny still records when she feels like hurting, and when she does harm herself. 'It's like a diary,' Franny says.

The impact of challenging behaviour is profoundly life changing, and the result of panicking can exacerbate the seriousness of the situation. So when Franny notices she is becoming worried or anxious, when things are not going too well at school, you will see her with her elastic bands listening to loud music. Her art becomes more strident and the colours bolder. She has just joined a running club and is meeting new people.

It is easy to forget what we have learned. Sometimes it is the absence of a thing that is more harmful than the presence of a thing: when Franny is doing well, when school hasn't noticed any meltdowns for a few weeks, when John and Lynne and Molly have said farewell to Mary, it will be possible to overlook the things needed to keep Franny (and themselves) on the straight and narrow. People might forget to talk. They might forget strategies. It is only when a challenging behaviour reappears that they will dust off proven strategies once more. We who support children or adults with behaviour we find challenging should not assume the individual is regressing; it is more likely we have temporarily forgotten to do what we know works.

By the time we complete our brief work with Franny, we have learned a good deal about our own limitations: sometimes, the best we can hope for is not to solve challenging behaviour but to understand the person more clearly. Lynne and John are both frustrated that Franny still self-harms (and Molly still believes a more robust consequence might be enough to 'snap her out of it') but they take some comfort from the fact this is at a much-reduced rate and is not a significant part of her life.

Franny herself has learned a great deal about growing up, and says she now has more 'good days than bad' (she has graphical evidence to show this). Franny said there are days when ice-cubes and elastic bands are not enough: hurting herself still makes her feel real. 'People worry this is about suicide,' Franny said, 'but it never is. This is about knowing I'm alive.'

QUESTIONS ABOUT *FRANNY: BEING THERE AND DOING MORE*

- Behaviour is a message that we can understand.

- This understanding may mean we have to alter or amend how we organise our relationships, our expectations and our own behaviour.

- Understanding means we can create places that fit better with what the person needs.

- It is easy to forget how far we have come. Take time to celebrate your successes. Take time to record what works. Don't panic.

CHAPTER 8

Hits Happen

Keeping Things Together when Things go Wrong

A good mosaic of strategies tells us how to avoid or amend conflict and confrontation and how to offer alternatives to challenging behaviour, but it should also tell us how to respond when incidents occur. This would be a poor book if it did not include strategies for emergency situations, even though we know avoiding a crisis is the best strategy. We should plan to be proactive but we would be foolish not to prepare for emergencies. Responding should reinforce the alternative behaviour and minimise the severity of challenging behaviour.

This chapter considers how we might plan to respond *following* challenging behaviour: we call these reactive strategies. There are endless ways of resolving an emergency that do not require children or adults being restrained, harmed or punished by those who truly should know better. This chapter presents just some of the alternatives to physical restraint.

I do not teach physical restraint techniques or interventions because there are *plenty* of alternatives to physical restraint techniques. Besides, I do not own a tracksuit or t-shirt with the name of a company earning money from teaching people how to restrain vulnerable people.

Reactive strategies must complement the individual's mosaic of proactive strategies. For example, if proactive strategies work to improve rapport and communication, a reactive strategy involving restraints and withholding loved activities will undermine proactive work. Restraints teach all manner of unhelpful things about power relationships. We cannot justify these just because a situation is dangerous. Dangerous behaviour does not warrant dangerous behaviour. Dangerous behaviours require greater creativity, greater understanding, greater choice and greater compassion, not less. We cannot at times predict emergencies – emergencies are cascading threads of unexpected chaos – but we can plan and practise how to respond to them should they occur.

As noted in the last chapter, reactive strategies are not intended to teach new skills – that is not their purpose. Some authors and practitioners do not consider reactive strategies to be interventions at *all* because their purpose is so modest. Reactive strategies are not big and they are not clever. The sole purpose of reactive strategies is to resolve a crisis swiftly, painlessly and positively, ending a difficult situation with dignity and relationships intact.

Good reactive strategies do not punish or threaten anyone and we are neither obliged to jump on anyone nor escort them away. Person-centred reactive strategies do not rupture hope or break trust or compromise quality of life by claiming to calm a child or adult by robbing them of choice or control or dignity. Reactive strategies call for clarity, calmness and choice. Reactive strategies buy people time to calm and resolve conflicts.

Reactive strategies must:

- be informed by the findings of the person-centred functional assessment summary statement

- be agreed by everyone involved – including the individual wherever possible

- reduce the risk of harm to all involved whilst increasing fast resolutions

- set out a range of gradient strategies for preventing, minimising or managing the behaviour of concern (see below)

- specify what behaviour they will be used with, where they will be used, how they will be used, how they will be recorded, and contain a plan to *reduce* their use over time

- emphasise communication solutions
- be discussed, practised and fine-tuned using role-play
- be reviewed after every use.

Strategies need to set out how to fix what has been broken. Reactive strategies describe how people should repair ruptured relationships.

The breakdown of trust is inevitable if restraints are used. Restraining someone will change your relationships with them and make no mistake, their use will change you. With each hold you bind yourself to a different future relationship.

Ask yourself:

- Is this emergency strategy something you would enjoy experiencing yourself?

- Is this something your two-year-old child, your partner or your grandparents would enjoy?

If the answer is no, I would humbly suggest it is not good enough for the child or adult you are supporting.

Upstream Investment

If the summary statement shows that a potentially harmful behaviour is predicted by a less impactful behaviour, reactive strategies should be designed to resolve the less impactful behaviour. By identifying the chain of behaviours that can often lead to serious challenging behaviour we can focus on intervening on these 'pre-cursor behaviours'. You do not ignore minor behaviours unless you know doing so is safe, and will not escalate into more impactful behaviour (LaVigna and Willis, 1997).

Reactive strategies can be useful by specifying intervention phases:

- Stage One describes low-arousal situations (i.e., the person is a little agitated or upset: Stage One strategies might involve active listening or diverting the person to a neutral or preferred activity).

- Stage Two describes specific strategies to more impactful pre-cursor behaviours of concern (i.e., the person swears, or bangs furniture, so the Stage Two strategies might involve novel stimulus (see below) – changing the environment, going someplace else, changing people around the person, leaving them to themselves where safe to do so).

- Stage Three describes specific strategies for the most serious behaviours. Some potential strategies are set out below.

If physical restraints are custom and practice it is useful to explore ways to reduce the duration and frequency of restraints by refocusing efforts on identifying, practising and implementing Stage One and Stage Two approaches. The reduction of restraints should be a primary goal for practice leadership (Deveau and Leitch, 2018).

It takes less effort and is less aversive *for everyone* to respond early. In the illustration in Figure 8.1, it would be most effective to defuse things when the individual vocalises. In this example, we might actively listen to what the person is saying through their vocalising.

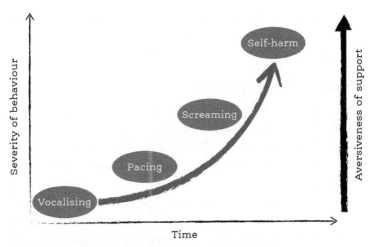

FIGURE 8.1: ONE THING LEADS TO ANOTHER

Being 'reactive' to these pre-cursor behaviours alleviates the need for more aversive or directive support later in the chain. We use the least damaging strategy first. Always.

This is common sense only if we assume some people do not actively enjoy using aversive and directive styles of support. I have observed people ignore minor behaviours in order to be able to respond to more challenging behaviour. Perhaps they mistakenly believe this is their job, or more charitably, they just do not see minor behaviours as potential predictors of more seriously harmful behaviours later in the day.

KEY POINTS FROM *UPSTREAM INVESTMENT*

- It is best not to wait for a crisis to come to you.
- It is best to practise reactive strategies.
- It is best to use reactive strategies during low-impact behaviours that could easily escalate if not addressed.
- If physical restraints are part of everyday support, what steps are being taken to make this not the case?
- What alternatives to physical restraints exist?
- Are physical restraints the least aversive option available?

Looking After One Another Takes Practice

When we experience challenging behaviour it is likely we will be frightened, horrified or fearful about the impact on ourselves as well as the impact on the individual. We may not think logically. It is as if a primitive version of ourselves pushes us aside to take control to ensure our safety. This is why practising the reactive strategies is so vital. Being confident about what is expected of us may increase our competence.

It is a big ask to expect someone to think well of a person who has just punched them. So an incredibly important element of any reactive strategy is specifying the support *you* can expect to receive during or following the incident. How we support one another during and following a crisis is a measure of competence.

Ensuring people are as well as can be expected following difficult situations is often called debriefing. In debriefing we discuss what happened and why, and most importantly, learn lessons to apply the next time. Debriefing is not about blame but about ensuring people are safe and well, discovering ways of coping in a crisis, and reviewing how people communicate before, during and following an incident. How people feel matters and ensuring they are able to express their concerns is vital.

An incident of serious challenging behaviour might result in post-traumatic stress. This means focusing on one-off debriefs is likely to not be sufficient support. Ongoing conversations are required and this means a healthy, competent and enabling culture should be the goal of any practice leadership role. We must take good care of those who do the supporting and the caring. But the reality is debriefing and ongoing support for people is something that often only happens to other people.

> **KEY POINTS FROM *LOOKING AFTER ONE ANOTHER TAKES PRACTICE***
>
> - It is best not to wait for a crisis to come to you.
> - It is best to practise reactive strategies.
> - It is best to use reactive strategies during low-impact behaviours that could easily escalate if not addressed.
> - If physical restraints are part of everyday support take steps to make them not necessary.
> - List alternatives to physical restraints – strategies that divert or avoid are best.
> - Ensure less aversive reactive strategies are used before you discuss the need for physical restraints.

Principles of Reactive Strategies

Reactive strategies should not punish. Punishing here could mean withdrawing activities or opportunities, or perhaps imposing a cost on the individual ('You've lost your trip out!'). Each human finds different experiences aversive, cruel or punishing, and what one person adores another might hate. For example, one person might find prison to be terribly rewarding, another will find it terribly punishing. Punishment is one of the least effective approaches to teaching. The argument for avoiding punishment is an argument for not causing damage to the person now and tomorrow. Punishment is tantamount to abuse. Abuse experienced in childhood seldom ends: it rolls down the years like pouring rain, flooding a life.

Punishing others can be addictive. Punishment is not as effective as other methods and it is often prohibited by professional, ethical and legal restrictions across the world. Despite this, we humans seem to cling to punishment as a method of teaching a person a lesson (even if it does not seem to work). We cling to it in movies, books and in society. Punishment is a trope we find hard to rewrite.

Before we consider some reactive options, we would do well to highlight a fundamentally important principle. It is a bête noire of many of the people I admire. In a crisis situation, just when everyone is exhausted and you start to wonder just how the hell you ended up in a situation where everyone is fighting for control, some bright spark will remind you, loudly, of the importance of not 'giving in'. But 'Do not reinforce challenging behaviour!' is a poor mantra to follow. It would be so *easy* to just end this situation by doing what the person was asking for in the first place, you think. And is not the job to help someone calm down rather than tell them off? It is so confusing! The person has a point – if you give in, and allow the person what they want, won't that *increase* the behaviour in the future?

Let me assure you the answer is no, *provided* the person has other ways of achieving the same outcome at *other* times not associated with the challenging behaviour. Resolving a crisis by giving the person what they are asking for is a sensible strategy. (Negotiation has saved numerous lives in human history. It makes sense to want to live another day.)

If the only time the person gets attention is following an outburst we might increase the possibility of the person 'selecting' the behaviour to gain attention *but* good support ensures the person gains attention unconditionally at other times. Doing so *weakens* specific functional relationships between challenging behaviour and attention by making attention more easily available for other behaviours.

More simply, if the only time I get a cup of tea is when I scream, sure I will scream each time I want tea. But learning to fix myself a cup of tea whenever I want means the unique relationship between screaming and tea is broken. Why scream when I have been taught to get tea myself whenever I want?

Thus we do not need to be so concerned about reinforcing challenging behaviour when we are working to resolve a conflict. In a conflict it is fine to give a cup of tea or whatever it is the person needs to resolve the crisis if it is safe to do so. This liberates us from tying ourselves in knots trying to avoid reinforcing behaviour. Reinforcement is one thing but resolution is another (LaVigna, 1995; Osgood, 2004).

For example, if a child self-harms to gain attention, to resolve the self-harm we often *need* to give attention to keep the child safe. We should thus focus on providing attention to the child when the self-harm does not occur and in a manner that is as powerful as when we give it following self-harm.

KEY POINTS FROM *PRINCIPLES OF REACTIVE STRATEGIES*

- Reactive strategies should not punish anyone: the cost of doing so is prohibitive.
- It is OK to give the person what they are asking for.

Some Suggested Strategies

The point of the strategies below is to buy everyone time to calm, reset and move on in order to normalise exchanges and support. These strategies simply distract or divert a person. In a crisis, the chances are no one is good at listening because they are upset, so where the strategies below make mention of speaking, remember communication is more than words: gestures, signs, facial expressions or symbols can often be used to negate the need to use words. For example, to communicate you understand your presence is making the situation worse, you don't talk, you simply remove yourself. If your *presence* is needed to resolve a crisis, just turn up and be present. Let your behaviour communicate.

Off-the-peg strategies often fit no one and the following suggestions will need to be adjusted, taken up, let down or trimmed according to the individual. Like all support strategies, reactive supports need to be tailored to the individual. Don't even attempt these unless you know the person very well and know what does not work.

Don't Say 'No' Until You've Tried 'Yes'

If it is safe to do so, give the person what they are asking for. Being listened to is powerful, but actually being given what you were asking for all along might come as such a shock challenging behaviour ceases momentarily. This approach is simply about giving rather than taking, even in a crisis. *Especially* in a crisis.

Don't Take Until You Have Given

When Steve Jobs and Apple introduced the iPad and iPhone, little did they realise they had created whole new categories of much-loved items parents and staff could threaten to remove: 'OK, Bob, *now* you've lost your iPad!' Like all instinctive behaviours, this removing of a much-loved item is counter-productive in the long term and says more about our need to feel in control than just about anything I could write.

'Don't tell them what you love else they'll make you earn it,' has been heard, I suspect, in more than one institution, and translates as, 'Hide your preferences from those who use them to get you to comply' while, 'Have it then, I don't care,' has been heard in too many homes, my own included, and can be translated as, 'Don't value anything others can deny you.'

As the best support worker I ever met explained to me long ago when I was so full of myself, 'We need to give to people what is rightfully theirs. We have no right to take from people what matters to them, no matter how good that taking away makes us feel about ourselves.' That, reader, is why I married her.

Increase Rather than Decrease Choice

Choice is one of the first victims of a crisis. Give the individual choices that help resolve the conflict. Offer conversations not controls, and provide options not blind alleys.

Given many individuals have been showing challenging behaviour for many years you might be forgiven for believing that having their choices limited would have taught them the error of their ways by now. Yet they persist in challenging. Therefore limiting choices and options may not be helpful. How about we rewrite the script to ensure we maintain or increase choice rather than limit it?

Of course the individual in crisis might be there simply because there is too *much* choice. In such circumstances removing some options may contribute to the individual resolving their own crisis by making the contexts easier to comprehend. The analogy is that of a motorway. When things are going well, when there are no roadworks or potholes, you can drive down any lane you want, but when there are problems on the road you might want to slow down and use the single available lane.

Apologise

Let me be honest with you. I have personally contributed to dozens of meltdowns, moments of challenging behaviour and conflicts, simple through not paying adequate attention to those around me. A comment, a joke, a sigh, a body posture, a suggestion, a frown – anything – might act as a predictor to challenging behaviour.

Saying 'sorry' can go a long way to resetting a situation. An authentic 'sorry' defuses many sorry situations. Saying 'sorry' is a promise. It means I will do my best to avoid the situation arising again. But if I keep saying 'sorry' whilst setting up situations leading to problems, no matter how heartfelt my 'sorry' is, it will lose its power. I will not be believed. This applies to individuals, teams and services.

'I was wrong' is a powerful and under-used phrase. Saying 'sorry' is the first stage of reparations and repairing a puncture in our relationship. To inflate our punctured relationship, I need to fix the hole before I put in air.

A Little out of Left Field

Also known as novel stimuli, challenging behaviour can often be paused by something unexpected occurring. If we know the person enjoys jokes, even when they are angry, then inserting a joke or a wry observation at a crucial juncture can sometimes defuse or distract them. Few people like jokes about themselves, so steer clear of quips that can be taken as a personal insult.

Singing a favourite song, falling to the floor faking a heart attack, asking an odd question ('Whatever happened to the rap version of the Gettysburg Address of 1863?'), farting, dancing, laughing suddenly, passing comment on someone else's dress-sense, hairstyle or footwear choices ('By all that is Holy, what is he *wearing?* 1967?'), bursting into tears, turning the lights on or off, jumping on the sofa, singing a hymn, running around the room, praying, fighting off non-existent bees, screaming in pain and claiming a penalty from a non-existent referee, praying for rain during a thunderstorm, phoning up to order in food, making a cup of tea, are *all* examples of novel (or new and unexpected) stimuli. The more left field the better.

The key point here is novelty. We need to ensure we do not fall into tired old ways of repeating our novel stimuli so often that they fail to be surprising, merely dull. In this way a good novel stimuli is like a long-lasting happy marriage in that it is important to avoid predictability, and to keep coming up with new ways to surprise one another. Only not so it causes a *real* heart-attack.

Take the Person Seriously

Active listening takes practice and a moment to work. Not listening takes hours to unpick.

Staff cannot actively listen if they are on their phones or so busy there is no time to pay attention to the people they are paid to support. Pay attention and respond early. Actively listen to what the person means, not just what they say. Being aware of the individual's 'mood' can avert many a crisis.

Share

It is absolutely fine to share how you feel. 'This is frightening, can you help?' may be enough to give pause. 'How did we fix this last time?' is an honest question to ask, and prompts the person to remember solutions.

It is often assumed the role of staff in a crisis is akin to the supposed role of a parent overseeing a child having a meltdown, but good parents do not get into a battle of control, they get in a confluence of choices. It is far better to enable self-control than exert control. Try honestly sharing your own concerns or hopes about a situation.

You May Not Have to Be Alone

Interdependence is far more rewarding than independence, and in a crisis, if they are available, it is utterly permissible to ask for another person to come and resolve situations that have got out of hand. A *change* of face can at times makes all the difference, and does not mean a *loss* of face. The individual might welcome such a de-escalation of a situation, too.

Many years ago in parts of the Indian sub-continent villagers seeking to capture monkeys filled baskets with fruit. The basket was tied to a tree. Monkeys would usually appear and insert a hand to get the fruit, but the hole in the basket was only big enough for a monkey's hand, not a monkey's hand holding fruit. Smart monkeys would let go the fruit in order to escape approaching humans, whereas those who were not so smart would not let go the fruit for anything (it's a free lunch!), and so found themselves tethered to the basket and so easily captured. If our need to be in control of difficult situations ourselves outweighs our ability to ask for support we fall into the not so smart category, unfortunately. Best let go of that particular fruit.

Diversion

My own favourite diversion is to ask, just as the person is mid-challenge, 'After we're done here, shall we go out for food?'

I have no reliable data on this but my impression is that this works more often than it does not *especially* if the person likes going out for a meal. People may continue to shout as they get their shoes on but they are heading in the right direction.

I once observed the strange spectacle of a support worker being shouted at by an angry child over *where* to go to buy ice-cream as part of a de-escalation. The support worker did not care about being shouted out (why would she *bother* to speak of 'appropriateness' and thus escalate the child into a rage once more?) but did care about getting out, changing the scene and buying ice-cream.

Eat Your Peas (Find What Brings You Together Not What Tears You Apart)

My children loved a particular book when they were growing up: a book that contained a secret message that every behaviour advisor should read. The book is written by Kes Gray and Nick Sharratt and is called *Daisy: Eat Your Peas.* (2009). In this masterpiece are a Child, a Mother, and a vegetable. (You can likely tell where this is headed.) The Mother wants the Child to eat her peas but the Child *hates* peas. Mother is insistent, because peas are green and green is good. Mother, being a wise robotic behaviour practitioner, seeks to encourage her daughter to eat her peas by way of complex bribery – if the Child eats her peas there is no end to what Mother will give her. After terribly entertaining exchanges between Child and Mother, and following ever more ridiculous inducements, it is the Child who resolves the conflict by pointing out that if they *both* simply ditched vegetables and opted to eat ice-cream, why, the battle would be over. In a crisis, there are worst things to do than finding what brings you together rather than tears you apart.

Ask and Be Honest

For some people, simply asking them to help you help them is all that is required: 'Can you help me?' or 'How can I help?' is all it takes to stop a crisis.

Swop Roles, Share Responsibilities

In a crisis we often adopt roles, and sharing the responsibility of a role that stipulates a responsibility to resolve issues might offer a momentary break in the unfortunate series of events obliging you both to tumble towards an unhappy ending.

As an example, let me introduce you to a young gentleman called Mo, a young man who taught me a great deal. Mo liked things done in a certain way. This included car journeys. When Mo travelled from home to his employment he preferred to travel a certain route. When traffic lights or delays happened Mo would often shout, hit out or try to wrench the steering wheel from the facia whether the driver was in the way or not.

We knew Mo wanted to be considered a grown-up (although he was in his early twenties, being 'grown up' meant a lot to him), and so we swopped roles. When approaching a delay during the journey, staff would 'act' in a frustrated manner, saying things like, 'Oh, for heaven's sake, this is annoying, look! Ugh! I'm getting angry! Hurry up!' whereupon Mo adopted 'a grown-up' stance, urging staff to, 'Stay calm, it can't be helped, we'll get moving soon. Shall I put the radio on for you? Remember your breathing.' In fact, Mo became the support staff and gave us suggestions we had previously shared with him.

We were very content with this terribly clever and enabling reactive strategy until one day Mo and his staff encountered a *long* line of traffic, and caught sight of an Air Ambulance landing in the road a mile or so ahead. The support worker knew it was time for an award-winning performance. He swore, he cursed, he banged the steering wheel, and he blamed the other drivers for the accident. Mo looked at his support worker aghast, reached over to pat his back and gently chided him, 'How could you? Someone could be hurt!' The support worker apologised. 'I'm sorry,' he said to Mo. 'I should think so, too,' Mo told him.

PRN

PRN is taken from the Latin *pro re nata* meaning *as circumstances arise*. (Some ideas about challenging behaviour are ancient.) In practice this means medication is given to help calm the person, but if the person is sufficiently calm to take medication they are sufficiently calm to chat or employ self-calming strategies. PRN medication, like all support strategies, must have a clear plan for when it is appropriate. If the plan is clear, there can be no doubt about how it is used.

It is important to discuss any reduction of such (usually psychotropic) medication with a variety of people and have firm plans for alternatives to support transitions from PRN medication to different strategies.

Use What the Person Can Do, Not What They Can't

For Mo, reactive strategies focused on what he could do as a means to divert himself away from more serious behaviours to less impactful ones.

Mo did not contain his anger to car journeys. At home he would sometimes become angry. (A common predictor was miscommunication and not being given time to make sense of what was being said. Seeing others getting attention from staff or family also made things difficult.) Mo would bite his hand or try to hit others. We knew that Mo would also vent his frustrations by kicking the hell out of garden bushes and swearing. Garden bushes seemed able to take a beating better than us, and did not bruise as much as Mo's hand.

The strategy began when Mo bit his hand or went to hit others. People would say, 'You're angry', then 'Want to kick?' and most often Mo would rage into the garden following the support worker. At times it felt a little like being chased. Replacing a rhododendron was easier than mending a person. Swearing together was a chance to bond, learn amazing new words, slowly calm, laugh at our ridiculous inventive obscenities, put the world to rights, and validate Mo's frustrations without validating the behaviour.

Back Off

It is important to remember that the only direction for someone once they are aroused is down. Time is your greatest friend. The person might well calm more quickly if you are not around. Leaving people to their own devices and calming strategies is often under-used.

But if we are present, our job is to quicken de-escalation, nothing more and nothing less. And so we may feel compelled to do something. Doing nothing beyond walking away is doing a great deal.

Life is too interesting and too much fun to spend over-long in a crisis. Which might mean those who are in crisis a lot may lack other interesting and fun things to do. Challenging behaviour is a small part of a very big life so we should not lose perspective. A crisis involving challenging behaviour will pass. But if a crisis is everyday, then something is fundamentally wrong with how that individual is supported (Pitonyak, 2007).

Give

If we know the person has preferred items (a soft toy, a favourite song, a preferred drink, a snack) then giving it to the person without saying a word is often sufficient to cause a break in challenging behaviour. The benefit of this is realised when the next time the person is in crisis they may look toward you hopefully. You may even be able to ask, 'Shall we get you ...?' and the person might agree to accompany you from the conflict area to a safe space to collect the item. This is a sign of a good rapport.

Sshh

There is a time to speak, show or guide, and there is a time to shut up. Might the individual interpret your 'counselling' as nagging? Try silence, try non-verbal communication. Reminding a child in a crisis that their behaviour is unacceptable may simply escalate the situation or prolong it. It is inevitable we want to feel in control but letting our primitive take over is not control. In a crisis, less communication is sometimes better communication. This seems to be a fairly common strategy much beloved of parents of autistic children: they have learned less verbal communication is *better* communication.

Tell

Some individuals respond well to being told what to do when they are upset. It is generally helpful to divert an individual onto an activity they like, a location they enjoy, or to go to a person with great rapport. Sometimes, Mo would welcome others saying, 'Mo, please just sit down'; depending how good a rapport that person had with Mo, he would usually do so.

Incompatibility

It is very difficult to pull your hair out if you are pulling the fur from a soft toy or brushing your hair. Topographically incompatible behaviours are behaviours that mean another behaviour is impossible to perform. It is hard to shout whilst taking a deep breath, for example (but you can go try). It is hard to spit when you are laughing. It is hard to shout 'no' when you are saying 'yes'.

One individual scratched the palms of her hands with her nails when she was anxious. The reactive strategy was for her to hold a preferred drink in one hand, a preferred soft toy in another, whilst she interacted with people who worked to help her feel less anxious. Scratching was thus not possible. No instructions were given. The preferred items were simply offered to her.

Know What Your Body Is Communicating

How we stand, how we act, and our expressions, are often as important as what we say and do. In a crisis our body language says more than we might imagine so be aware that our position and physical attitude can contribute to rapid resolutions or sudden escalations. Folding our arms might make us appear closed-off and not open to people. Not standing with our hands on our hips helps as does avoiding a stance reminiscent of a sailor navigating choppy seas off the Cape of Good Hope. Some people need the reassurance you are a reliable captain in a heavy storm, and such stances might contribute to them seeing you appear to be in control, and that is just what they need. But for others, it comes across as a threat.

Do not point fingers and do not loom unless you know it is what the individual needs to help them calm quickly. If you feel tense, relax, and your fists will likewise unwind – your head might well follow, because mental attitude often follows physical attitude.

Calming Mindfully

If during the course of an ordinary life we practise relaxation or calming skills, even mindfulness, during a crisis we can make use of our learning; practice makes perfect and having the skills to calm or think differently about our situations is like carrying our own personal safe space around with us.

Mindfulness is old as the hills though it has recently grown in popularity. In mindfulness we do not try to control feelings or thoughts, we simply note they are there. Thoughts and feelings arise and fade away. Feelings *will* pass: fears, hopes and anger do disappear. We can choose to respond to these or not. By noting them we do not stop them, but they lose their power to order us about.

We can – from one perspective – dissociate ourselves from those feelings. We can sense the impact of those feelings but know they will pass. It sometimes helps to focus attention on our breathing or on the soles of the feet (Singh *et al.*, 2007). Mindfulness can be done practically anywhere and requires no resource other than time and someone to help us learn it. Mindfulness is a useful skill to teach everyone: children and adults, people using services, people providing services. It is often especially useful for parents who more than anyone know the definition of *stress*.

Progressive Relaxation

Franny is learning progressive relaxation when she is not angry or in a crisis. Learning to relax *can* be used when she is angry, however. Progressive relaxation involves the relaxing of different groups of muscles and paying attention to how that feels. There are usually set sequences to how this is taught, and for a helpful overview of this and other relaxation techniques, see Payne (2000). Franny is learning to sense the difference between tense muscles and relaxed muscles. Such body knowledge might contribute to Franny identifying when she is tensing up, and so actively relaxing. Such tense–release learning is not for everyone, especially if they have hypertension, heart issues or experience hallucinations.

In summary, a good support mosaic *never* relies on reactive strategies to bring about change because reactive strategies are not intended to avoid or replace challenging behaviour. Reactive strategies simply keep everyone safe and resolve a crisis. Reactive strategies are not big and they are not clever but they can make or break a relationship.

KEY POINTS FROM *HITS HAPPEN: KEEPING THINGS TOGETHER WHEN THINGS GO WRONG*

- Never rely on reactive strategies.

- The strategies in this chapter are not intended to teach anything other than people can help resolve as well as start conflicts.

- Reactive strategies bring about temporary reductions in challenging behaviour and are, perhaps, all the more insidious for this: relying on reactive strategies can blindside us to the real work of teaching alternative skills.

Keeping Your Human Well-Nourished: Ray

One gentleman I worked with lived in a hospital and was often put into arm restraints called splints following self-harm. The splints were made from thick yacht-sail like canvas cut into rectangles, with seams through which long metal strips were threaded: they would be fastened about each arm by Velcro fastenings, like straightjackets for arms. These splints stopped Ray from being able to bend his arms and hit his own head: they also, as a by-product, made it impossible for him to use the toilet – so he was dressed in toileting pads. They made it impossible for him to feed himself or drink – so staff fed him and gave him sporadic sips of tea. He also wore a padded helmet just in case he did hurt himself. He wore splints and a helmet for most of the day. He did nothing: he paced, he sat, and he vegetated.

In conversation with staff, it was told how this man would sometimes be stripped and made to stand in the hospital courtyard, where he would be hosed down in cold water to stop his self-harm. Ten years of this treatment hadn't stopped his self-harm, and his trust of humans was as rare as the days his face wasn't bruised. The trouble with relying on reactive strategies is that all too easily one thing leads to a worse thing – because reactive strategies can never lead to a long-term resolution, people increase the punishment.

In discussions, it was apparent that if Ray was busy he tended not to harm himself. It was also clear staff had little time to keep Ray busy. They knew of no realistic alternative to splints, they said. When Ray wore splints, he couldn't hurt himself, and this meant staff could get on with their day.[1]

Regarding Ray's self-harm and Ray's life, we discovered the following:

- Ray could hit his head up to 72 times a minute (from records and observation).

- Ray's self-harm was predicted by Ray crying and vocalising, which was predicted by nothing happening: Ray was not engaged for over 90 per cent of his time.

- Ray's injuries caused him a lot of sinus pain.

- Ray loved tea and soft drinks, he enjoyed food, but he adored going for walks. He was on a behaviour programme: regulated tea, limited meals, a walk once every two days (staff permitting).

- He'd been institutionalised as a young man.

- Staff were as institutionalised as Ray.

During our exploring we also discovered that when he was feeling pre-disposed to self-harm, and before he had splints put on in the morning by his staff, Ray would seek out his helmet and his splints and wear them.

Now often the splints had to be washed overnight: to accommodate this the metal strips could be removed. Sometimes a strip would be lost. Ray had learned over the years that wearing splints meant he couldn't hurt himself.

---

1 Yes, you're right! An elephant in the room is *so what was their day about if not supporting Ray?*

In the same way we do not drive through red lights at traffic signals even though we could, Ray did not hit his face when he wore the splints – even when the splints had no constraining metal strips. Ray could scratch his ear and hair, rub his nose, but because he wore the splints, he did not harm himself.

The solution for this rather wonderful but wounded gentleman involved escaping the hospital through creation of a person-centred plan, living in a home where he had his own room, his own routine and his own name. It involved teaching him to meet his needs in other ways. It involved recruiting staff that were bothered about long-term solutions not a short-term gain. We addressed quality-of-life issues, contributed to a person-centred plan and conducted a person-centred functional assessment.

Some days Ray did not reach for his splints (sans metal strips). But he always knew where the splints (and the helmet) were should he feel the need. Slowly, we cut down the splints, and reduced the helmet. Within a few weeks Ray's splints consisted of sweatbands, and his helmet was a baseball cap. Most days Ray did not need to wear these signs that told him he *could not* hit himself, but sometimes he did need to wear them and that was OK. He was terribly busy with his new home and his new activities and people who seemed to be bothered about him.

The people supporting Ray in his new home had their own support plan to remember why Ray must know sweatbands and baseball caps were available; they needed to be able to remember why an active and meaningful life was important for Ray not to hurt himself. Their support plan included:

- working in teams to share ideas, learning from near misses

- working together to keep learning alive about Ray and about what good support looked like

- working together to share the demands of supporting Ray and to talk about how hard it was

- having telephone support 24/7 wherever they were

- learning mindfulness in order to stay calm and positive

- having a network of colleagues who could step in at short notice.

David Pitonyak reminds us that knowing someone is a vital component of being considered human, and this book urges us to get to know the person we support – warts and all, for good and bad, in sickness and in health. Knowing someone well means knowing not only the apparently important things to others (a doctor needs to know height, weight, blood pressure, your history and lifestyle) but the important things to that person: their identities, their loves, their dislikes, their stories.

David Pitonyak says we all need someone to hold our stories because it helps us belong to one another. He notes hundreds of thousands of words are written about people with IDD or autistic people over the course of their lives, very few of which tell the story of their life. I would in part tell the story of the lives of my four children through tall tales and photographs, through sharing stories, tears and laughter, not through descriptions of their medical histories. They do not have to be good to be loved.

They do not have to be skilled or talented to be heroes to me. We hold each other's stories – even the bits that are nightmares. Stories are to be told and shared; when we do, we share a little of the wonder we feel about others. Data are important, as are the stories about people. Pitonyak (2007) writes that for people with IDD, for too many autistic people, there are too few stories, too much paperwork.

KEY POINTS FROM *KEEPING YOUR HUMAN WELL-NOURISHED: RAY*

- Stories and data work well together in describing what matters to the person.
- Using behavioural science in person-centred ways can change lives for the better.
- Behavioural science can help the person become whoever they wish to become.

CHAPTER 9

What People have
Taught Me

The vernacular used by services for those with IDD or autistic people whose behaviour challenges is too often built upon an ancient language. Old ideas remain evident in current practice. We hear talk of behaviour management as opposed to good support, we hear talk of restraints not teaching, punishment and pathology not rapport and communication. I suspect services and special schools spend more each year on physical restraint training than on teaching staff how to communicate with those who are difficult to hear.

New words are deployed like bumper stickers to give the appearance of modernisation and person-centred principles, but such words are soon degraded and polluted because they adhere to old archaeology and antique ways of thinking: neologisms act as euphemisms for old practice. Services may not speak of physical restraint but instead talk of two-person escorts; they may not speak of punishing reprimands but may mention counselling someone about their behaviour after an incident (we can call that nagging; reminding someone how *bad* their behaviour is, how *bad* they are, and the degree of feigned disappointment others feel is not counselling. It just adds to everyone's trauma). Services may seldom speak of time-out but mention in passing the need for someone to calm down by reducing their choices in a quiet space. In some ways, challenging behaviour now means what problem behaviour meant, what abnormal behaviour implied: that the behaviour is the responsibility of the individual and their disability.

The last fifty years have seen significant and palpable improvements in the support of autistic people and those with intellectual and developmental disabilities, but there are too many places where the rhetoric of new approaches is used to obscure ancient prejudice. And the narrative is still too often about services and professionals, not people and families.

Your phone rings.

'Behaviour support, can I help?'

'We hope so. We've a person who is a *real* problem. He's costing us a fortune in staff and stress. Can you fix the problem?'

'Sure!'

'You can? Great!'

'A couple of questions first.'

'Fire away!'

'Have you a detailed person-centred plan to guide your work in delivering the life the person says is important to them? Does this plan outline what the person needs and wants, the practical steps to take, the type of communication that works best, the form of interaction the person welcomes? Do you keep your promises to deliver an interesting life supported by people with great communication and good rapport?'

'Yes!' (There is usually a pause at this point.) 'Actually no.'

'OK. Can you tell me why not?'

'Well...'

'Because if you're not following *best* practice, what the hell *are* you doing accepting money to support them?'

Our work must be technically robust and clinically valid – evidence based – but it must also be socially valid. It must be relevant to the delivery of a good quality of life, done in a way that is contextually sensitive and appropriate. Our suggestions must not ride roughshod over the person's dignity and choices. Our interventions must not act as the deliberate annulment of their future. If the ideas we are contributing are not good enough for *our* loved ones, they are not good enough for someone *else's* loved one. If they are not good enough for people surrounded by family and friends, they are not good enough for people who have nobody in their lives to speak on their behalf.

This is compassion as work, this is putting values into action. Our work must not be an act of collaboration with those seeking to maintain the status quo of poor support. We need more prophets describing a positive future, less profits turning humans into units of economic generation.

What people researching best practice and the most effective types of provision have taught me is as follows: we would do well to organise ourselves to deliver the life the person wishes, remembering that people change their minds about where they want to go *but that's OK*. I have been taught that the delivery of a good support system may well offset exotic communication. Knowing what the person needs for a good day tends to inform how we support people: if we're not doing what works for the person, what *are* we doing? I have been taught that if behaviour is reducing the quality of life of the person in terms of well-being, health and happiness, in terms of reducing opportunities to engage in a good life with good support in a place they enjoy, we should address these things through understanding what the challenging behaviour achieves, organise the environment to reduce events predicting challenging behaviour, teach the person alternative behaviours that achieve the same outcome, and fundamentally enable new ways of communicating.

The pearls of wisdom autistic people and those with IDD have taught me are significant. Most often it is important to turn up and shut up, and vital to avoid at all costs a sense of entitlement accruing from perceived expertise. We should avoid the seductive power of being a hero, and seek rather to be a host to learning. Behaviour usually holds a message we would do well to hear because behaviour is lawful even when awful.

Working with families has taught me that to know about positive behaviour support is not the same as doing it. A behavioural advisor who is not a practice leader – a doer rather than a talker – is as useful as a pair of inflatable armbands in a hurricane to people needing support. A good practitioner turns up at ungodly hours or whenever needed. A good practitioner never sends an assistant to collect data: they turn up themselves to hear stories whilst collecting data. A strategy provides a framework through which we can deliver support, but it is not the work. The job is not to write strategies but to spend time alongside people, working in partnership, in order to understand how better to support them.

Working with services, schools and professionals has taught me that a place not asking questions about how to work better is a place too complacent with their own expertise. Smug won nobody friends. In terms of services, as Herb Lovett said, anyone can put a grass skirt on a cow but it still won't hula. Some services are just not designed to deliver a good quality of life. The best practice leaders have taught me to opt for changing how things are done, not how things are spoken (Lovett, 1996). Finally, I have learned that upstream solutions are usually more help than downstream rescues because splashing about in the downstream shallows just gets everyone soaked.

What working with people has taught me is that we can often overlook the need for a place for everyone in finding the meaning of challenging behaviour and solutions to ameliorate its impact. We can amplify the crucial need to support parents and paid staff by embedding in our work a need to arrive at a description of our own support needs. Too often there is an assumption parents do not need sleep or time away or time as adults. Support staff too often surprise professionals or managers when they offer an opinion about the expectations being placed upon them. Too often parents and support staff are held up to ridicule or blame. Support staff can be fired and children removed from parents. But *really?* Better to ensure support staff and parents are fully supported to make often difficult or stressful situations a success.

In 'Exploring' we discovered the benefits of understanding why humans do what humans do. Knowing that if parents and support staff do not take care of themselves or are not well supported they will become tired, down-hearted and fatalistic, it is legitimate to wonder how support and nurturing is provided to them in order to avoid such exhaustion.

One of the contributions we can make is to ensure both parents and support staff are heard, are respected, and involved. Rather than berate people for failing to implement a strategy, perhaps we need to ensure the strategy is fit for purpose, fit for place, and has not failed the people doing a difficult job with little to show by way of thanks. The chapter 'The Elephants in the Room' should be reread whilst keeping parents and support staff in mind. The mosaic of proactive strategies in 'Doing More and Being There' can be used to organise support of parents and support staff.

Support strategies for people doing the hard work include:

- being able to express fears and doubts, to share ideas and suggestions

- having access to practical advice and reliable information from informed others

- being involved in key decisions that affect people

- building time for people to gather together to share

- access to training, knowledgeable people, respite and emotional support

- knowing what to do and who to turn to when things go wrong.

Often the support plans I see are not big and they are certainly not clever. They simply repeat what has not worked before only using different words. The plans focus on now – in keeping people safe by denying them a future – and few plans speak of what the challenging behaviour is saying, or what it means, or even why it is happening. Too many plans aim to make staff and families agents of conformity. Too many people with IDD whose behaviour challenges the system are living unnecessarily denuded lives and families are tired of fighting the same battle every time there is a new professional on the scene.

Bruno Schulz (1892–1942) was a Jewish-Polish man whose work I much admire. His life was arbitrarily ended by a robotic man who in all likelihood did not even know the name of the human he murdered in the street, let alone Schulz's artistic, teaching and writing gifts.

Sometimes I wonder what other gems Schulz might have placed in our hands to enjoy had he not on his way home from a bakery encountered a uniformed robot. In his *The Street of Crocodiles and Other Stories* (originally published in Polish in 1937), Schulz wrote, 'The days hardened with cold and boredom like last year's loaves of bread. One began to cut them with blunt knives without appetite, with a lazy indifference' (2008, p.19). Such days are not conducive to happiness but are common for autistic people or those labelled with IDD.

This small book about challenging behaviour is written in an informal manner to encourage us *all* to contribute to making days a little warmer and less boring for children and adults who rely upon us. Removing elephants in the room can give people space to breath. Understanding the message of the challenging behaviour can help our endeavours to better support the individual.

This little book asks us to nurture our human selves and be actively heedful to other humans, rather than robotic and indifferent to the meaning of the language of challenging behaviour. Such behaviour is *not* the determining aspect of anybody's life: challenging behaviour is simply a symptom of an unquiet life, of a fellow human in distress.

Keeping Your Human Well-Nourished: Harry

Robots can fall into tragic loops of logical error. If someone challenges to get attention, a robot will stop giving attention because 'we must not reinforce a problem behaviour'. If someone is thought to be obsessive about an activity or a thing or a person, a robot might decide it is 'in the person's best interest' to reduce access to that activity or person or thing. A human knows if we limit someone's access to a thing we make it more attractive, they want it all the more. To reduce an obsession we provide other interesting things the person enjoys or might learn to enjoy.

I was once working with a professional when he was asked to help a service stop the obsessive eating of someone the service supported. Harry was in his twenties, did not use words, was autistic, had severely limited eyesight, and had severe intellectual disabilities. He also grabbed at his food and he ate fast. We were told Harry was *obsessed* by food (though some of us just thought Harry was hungry, a side-effect of his medication and not having anything else interesting in his life). The professional decided the best thing to do was to remove Harry's plate of food after each mouthful so he wouldn't rush and choke.

That would slow him down, the professional told me.

'That will piss off Harry,' I suggested.

Dinner times suddenly became a lot more interesting. Soon, along with serving mediocre soggy pasta and cold congealed soup, there were second helpings of food fights and zesty desserts of wrestling. Each time Harry spied the hand of the professional reaching for his food he would attempt to simultaneously *bite* the hand that didn't feed him and run into the garden. It turned out Harry could run fast whilst eating, whilst *leaping* over staff, all without dropping a morsel.

The professional's well-intentioned intervention made Harry even *more* obsessive about getting his food while he had the opportunity. Not only was the professional's training about behaviour support out of date but his tiny human had not been nourished for years. Further, the professional said Harry's fixed ideas about food were evidence of his autistic nature, whereas the professional's fixed ideas were not: we live in a strange and remarkable world, as many autistic people might ruefully note.

Humans convinced the professional to try a number of ways of helping Harry *get* his food, *slow* down, and *learn* that meals were not opportunities for practicing the 110 metre hurdles. This is what we did:

- Harry liked water. After each mouthful we offered Harry the glass of water beside his plate. We did not speak. We simply showed Harry the glass. Harry put down his knife and fork in order to take a drink of water between mouthfuls of food. We broke up fast eating by encouraging naturally available options. (It also helped when we offered condiments. It helped to have small dishes of other foods that Harry could add to his plate.)

- Harry liked most people (though not people who stole his food). We asked different people to sit with Harry and talk to him about things Harry liked. This confused some people because they didn't *know* what Harry liked, so we suggested this would be the perfect opportunity to discover such things.

- For Harry, people were OK, but not as exciting as food or water. So to help people appeal to Harry, they would sneak small portions of food to Harry whilst smiling conspiratorially. Harry could not speak, but he recognised a good deal when he saw one, and his smile broke many hearts. Harry soon learned people gave him food (and which person gave him the nicest food) and who provided the more interesting conversation, and the better smiles. Harry's rate of eating slowed down. Soon many people began to like spending time with Harry and Harry cut them a break *provided they didn't steal his food.*

- We made sure Harry had opportunities to get snacks outside of meal times: he came to the table a little peckish but not ravenous. It turned out Harry was far happier eating a little often than eating a lot at meal times.

- We asked Harry if he would like to prepare meals and snacks. We did this by giving him opportunities to cook in the kitchen. Harry in the kitchen was a wonderful experience, though at times the kitchen might have felt it had survived a visit from an enthusiastic hurricane.

- We asked Harry if he would like snacks in his room. We did this by putting snacks in his room and gauging his response. Harry did like snacks in his room. Especially raw vegetables.

- We began to look at medication that did not make Harry constantly thirsty or hungry.

- We began to reset relationships between staff and Harry. We helped staff not be so demanding and directive, and be more social. This involved amending the staff rota a little to allow more time for being together.

- We taught the professional to nurture his human because it made life easier for everyone. And it meant for every other Harry the professional met, he might think in less robotic ways. It turns out one robot can cause a lot of damage to many people, but a tiny human goes a long way.

- There was a rumour that at the professional's retirement celebration some unhelpful behavioural advisor kept stealing the professional's plate of cake, asking, 'How does that *feel*, hmmm?' just to emphasise a point.

- At the end of all our endeavours a new manager at Harry's home thought Harry was getting far too personal a form of support. She withdrew the support strategies. She said it wasn't equitable with the type of support other people received. Instead of raising the quality of support she delivered to everyone, she lowered it to a minimum standard. It turns out inspectors and safeguarding authorities are quite happy with minimum standards, and they failed to see a problem when Harry received pretty shoddy provision. The new service manager mentioned that she *would* reinstate the support if the service received more money.

- We supported Harry to find a better, smaller and more person-centred place to live, because life is too short to spend it surrounded by people who are indifferent to your welfare: life is too precious to spend it with arseholes who are paid to do one thing but deliver another.

Harry teaches us two things. First, a placement in a service is not the same as living in a home. Second, one robot in a position of authority can in a single moment screw up months of human work.

The service Harry lived in was like several places I have worked in, in that they try to minimise risk from challenging behaviour by having guidelines for staff that in effect remove choice and dignity. One of the risk assessments told staff, 'Harry must be calm for three hours prior to going out' when in reality, Harry was *seldom* calm because he was *excited* about the prospect of going out. Denying Harry the chance to go out just made him even *less* calm.

Very few of us will be Buddha-like when facing our one trip out each week. The strategy did not serve Harry but it served the service's agenda of asking for more money due to increasing challenging behaviour.

Good support would enable Harry to go out often and go out now rather than wait for a perfect tomorrow. Good support ensures a quality of life is experienced as part of the support not as a consequence of an unreachable state of perfection. Harry will never be perfect because no one is perfect. But Harry, like the rest of us, is good enough and deserves to have what he needs. Plenty of unperfected people have the power to accuse others of not being ready, safe or perfect.

Robots make humans scratch their heads and despair. But the good news is robots can be reprogrammed. They can be worked around. We humans simply need to show robots alternatives to their pre-programmed ideas about what works and what is more effective.

We have to show robots the value of being more human. Even if that robot is a part of us.

KEY POINTS FROM *KEEPING YOUR HUMAN WELL-NOURISHED: HARRY*

- Focus on what the person can do rather than punishing them for what they cannot currently do.
- Focus on building new skills upon current abilities.
- Don't be satisfied with minimum standards.

CHAPTER 10

Afterword

What I Think when I Talk about Autism

There could be other books. (Think of this less as a threat and more a hopeful promise.) A book focused on positive behaviour support and practice leadership, for example, or one concerning how we might easily mend meltdowns without using physical interventions or dehumanising responses (this must include how we *feel* not merely how we think about facing challenging behaviour.)

These *possible* books might also explicitly consider autism. Because even in this book about challenging behaviour readers will have noticed an elephant in my room, namely, my infrequent use of the word 'autism': this is inevitable due to the fact that in our family autism is personal, and as the great Canadian poet Alden Nowlan (2004) noted when receiving a poem from his son, writing the personal is about the most meaningful thing a human can share with another. It takes gumption and authority.

Naturally this book mentions approaches to challenging behaviour that are applicable in autism because the approaches are (I hope) *human* friendly: they apply to people, because good behaviour support is much like gravity: no human is immune (no matter what they choose to believe). Humans are a diverse spectrum[1] of a species,

---

1   This suggests linearity – from 'very' to 'little', from 'tall' to 'short', for example, as if humans can be categorised so very simply. The reality is very different. 'Spectrum' doesn't have to mean a line; it can imply a continuum, such as in this case. Multi-axial imagery works better, I think, and avoids a sense we are each associated with quantifiable definitions and thus fixed for life. Saying an autistic person is at one point of a spectrum diminishes our capacity to understand the variations amongst people at 'the same place' on the spectrum, and so limits our understanding.

with both nuanced and significant identities and capacities: we share certain characteristics, for example, our ability to learn, to feel, to share, to belong, and their opposites. We have far more in common than some people would have you believe.

Wherever I go to talk or work regarding challenging behaviour, autism is mentioned. In response to *anything* I say concerning behaviour someone usually adds, 'In principle…but in autism?' One reason I struggle to respond is because it may be we are speaking at cross-purposes when discussing autism; it may be too personal, and it may be words have failed me: how can I speak of remarkable things, such as the variegated patterns of humanity, its diasporas of identities, whilst also suggesting we all have much in common, without offending those being or seeking unique identities?

To side-step miscommunication I have learned to suggest that if the principles of good behaviour support are truly person centred in their application, then elements can be applied to support individuals regardless of diagnosis, identity or attribute. Good practitioners are sensitive to individual preferences whilst using common principles of person-centred functional assessment and person-centred behavioural support. Person-centred support looks at individuals as whole people rather than diagnostic categories, even if diagnostic categories can teach us about *likely* commonalities.

Autism is a label that is applied to a diverse group of people sharing some commonalities, and it may turn out autism isn't one thing but many: autism is one thread of humanity that is present from childhood and continues throughout the person's life. We cannot cure autism. (There's a debate to be had about even assuming we should. Think of the implications of curing *any* part of humanity. Who judges, who decides, and who carries out such a final solution? Evolution seems to know what it is doing in producing such differences amongst humans.) Because autism – in its current definition – is a tall, wide, deep and many-coloured splendid thing, it is easy to spot these commonalities in some, more difficult due to its nuanced appearance in others.

It doesn't help that some diagnostic methods seem biased toward obvious behavioural or cognitive signs that are good often for males and not so great often for females: both are equal but different in terms of autism assessment. And then there are those who identify as neither – are diagnostic tools keeping up? (Only if our *recognition* of the need for more subtle ways to comprehend each other does.) The end result is that whilst plenty of young children are diagnosed early, many are not. There are times people are not diagnosed until some way through their lives, and some, not at all. Should every autistic individual be identified? Being diagnosed *should* enable support to be tailored, and the individual to have a foundation from which to build their identity, and it certainly may help others to understand a little more about the individual. We diagnose through observing behaviour. This is like commenting on the quality of the meal as we stand outside a restaurant.

As I write, people living in one county of the UK face a waiting list for a child's autism assessment through statutory services of thirteen months. That's pretty shoddy and inept, especially as it impacts the well-being not only of the child, but of families. Further, once a diagnosis is received the experiences of gaining insightful support are not uniform across the UK. It turns out there are deserts and forests across the land – of provision, expertise and vision. The autistic diagnosis is only the first hurdle in a steeplechase across such a landscape: the dangerous water jump on the second lap is getting information and support following that diagnosis.

Traditionally we say autism is present when we observe certain patterns of behaviour. Everyone we meet thinks they know about autism, even if it's rudimentary or stereotypes derived from the television show *The Big Bang Theory* or the film *Mary and Max*. No media representation can truly reflect people, only small bits of their experiences. Autism 'behaviours' vary depending on mental capacity, age, skills and opportunities offered. And it depends how much people trust the person assessing them.

One commonality across 'the autisms' is 'empathic capacity' (Delfos, 2005, p.84) – that is, the ease with which the individual relates to others. You see, one neurotribe[2] thinks the autistic neurotribe

---

2   Let's imagine humanity is made up of different groups who share ways of thinking and experience the world – think of a neurotribe as a community of experience, each sharing commonalities and preferences. People can each belong to many different tribes over their lives, I suspect. We can craft ourselves.

struggles with empathy, which is a bit rich given the track record of a lack of understanding common *across* neurotribes (Silberman, 2015). So autistic people are considered to lack empathy, which I'm sure you'll agree, shows a distinct lack of empathy, a problem with generalisation, and a lack of imagination, by those pointing accusing fingers. This is called the double-empathy problem (Milton, 2012): both autistic people and neurotypical struggle to empathise and understand one another.

Another thing people speak of as being a commonality in autism is an often *uneven* set of abilities: if we were to graph the different skills of children or adults, the diagram would seem a little 'spiky': great at this, not so great at that. An individual may be able to debate moral relativism but have trouble safely crossing a road. Such a profile may be extremely spiky in autistic individuals but to a lesser or greater degree the same thing is found in many humans. In autism, it's the *significance* of such differentials that matters.

We may all experience anxiety about social situations to some degree, but what is a lukewarm unpleasantness for some is a roaring broiling pot of horror for others. After a busy day filled with novel social situations, neurotypicals might relax in the peace and quiet of solitude, but many autistic people might collapse from exhaustion at trying to translate what the hell has occurred and what it means to be them.

Similarly, we may each have certain sensory preferences, but autistic people may not have an option but to feel their teeth are electrified when eating certain foods or textures. Neurotypicals might dislike certain smells or sounds, but an autistic person is hardwired to find them physically repulsive. Again, it's a matter of the magnitude.

For more than twenty years we've spoken of autism as one umbrella term to describe a *spectrum* of different *presentations*. We know each of these presentations *tends* to have characteristics justifying our use of the term 'autistic': these of course include differences from the abilities shown by others in terms of communication, social interactions and patterns of behaviour including cognitive behaviours, but they also very much seem to incorporate sensory processing. These have become known, for good or ill, as the *triad of impairments*. (There go the neurotribes again, labelling a difference as an impairment.)

Whether someone is intellectually gifted and eloquent, or has no speech and has severe IDD, we might see similar characteristics or commonalities through their behaviour.

Here's a conundrum: if the autistic child learns to behave in ways that are not considered 'autistic', are they autistic any longer? That is the claim of some behaviourists: to teach behaviours that mask or replace 'autistic' behaviours so well the child might not be considered autistic based on our assessment of autism as a collection of observable behaviours. But autism is so much *more* than observable behaviour: it is a way of thinking and experiencing the world (e.g., Grandin, 1995; Jackson, 2002). 'Autism' is a term that encompasses people with profound IDD, Nobel Prize winners, and everyone in between.

Whilst we might once have said the 'spectrum' of autism consisted of three distinct 'groups', today we think this is less absolute. Some find the 'three group' spectrum helpful in terms of identity:

- classic (or Kanner's) autism

- Asperger's syndrome

- atypical autism, sometimes confounded with pervasive developmental disorders.

Each 'type' has unique indicators though a person who has been diagnosed with one of these might appear little different from a person with another 'type' of autism, especially for support purposes (Wing, 1998). Therefore some ways of diagnosing autism have eliminated these three groups, combining them into a single 'autism'. This means that when we hear the word 'autistic', we might be speaking of divergent individuals: 'autistic' can cover a multitude of spiky profiles. Autistic people (like all humans) have variable attributes whilst also having commonalities. (People keep tinkering with the definitions, but the people being spoken of remain, and the experiences of their lives go on.)

Not all autistic people share the gifts outlined in Table 9.1, as not all those who are not autistic (neurotypicals) do, but Vermeulen (2001) provides a short and handy guide to what we might expect to encounter.

Table 9.1: Giftedness (adapted from Vermeulen, 2001, p.132)

Gifts of autistic and non-autistic people	
Autistic People	Non-Autistic People
Literal interpretation of information	Contextual interpretation (spirit of things)
Analytic thinking (not so integrated)	Integrated thinking (not so analytical)
Eye for details (misses big picture)	Eye for big picture (misses detail)
Concrete things and facts (vagueness not welcome)	Abstract things and vague ideas (not so good at facts, questions literalism)
Rule following	Living between the rules
Objectivity ('mind blindness')	Subjectivity ('theory-of-mind')
Realism ('what is')	Surrealism ('what is not')
Perfectionism ('binary – good or bad')	Flexibility ('shades of goodness')
Absolutes	Relativism
Calculations	Intuitive feelings

Vermeulen might be the first to acknowledge just how many exceptions we each know. And that's why I'm so cautious about talking about autism; the older I get the less certain I am of the ideas I grew up with.

When I was a child we had *nine* planets (poor Pluto got dumped from the club – if they can exclude a heavenly body, what chance have *I* got?). Also, in the good old days, I only had to contend with three dinosaurs – the hungry one with tiny paws, the veggie big one with that cool sail on its back, and the huge one with the massive tail stomping early humans. Now there are thousands of dinosaurs (and early humans weren't even around).

And that is why research goes on, to help us learn more evidenced accounts of why things are as they appear. There are always new things to discover and older lessons to remember. Ructions are inevitable.

We are some way from finding a simple and elegant explanation of what causes autism – perhaps there are, as Uta Frith suggests, long causal chains comprising many factors (Frith, 2003) that lead to a myriad of neurological changes that may be profound or mild in their effect on the person. Regardless of causes and processes, whether autism is one thing or many, the outcomes can be profound:

> My way of functioning has also meant that occasionally I find it difficult to show understanding of other people. I can't help thinking that people are rather pathetic in their need to be loved by everyone; that they are naïve not to be able to disregard their own feelings, to keep things and people apart, even. But usually I just feel sorry for them when they can't… But now I've realised I needn't be sorry for them, because they do gain something from what seems so troublesome to me. They think it's good to get so involved, and that people really are concerned about others. They perhaps even want to be drawn into conflicts and then complain about it, because they think it's just part of life. They don't always mean what they say: they can say something is upsetting when in fact they like it. (Gerland, 1997, pp.245–246)

What I think when I talk about autism is that my fragmentary account is only one pixel of a picture. My pixel has been drawn from memory, personal experience, practice and current research, and my pixel is being refreshed every moment. The *other* thing I think when I talk to others about autism is that for each account I hear people espouse I try to remain acutely aware of exceptions. When a neurotypical tells me autistic people do this or do that, I think the following: *neurotypicals are so obsessed with their limited interests in suggesting the autistic mind isn't good at empathy and communication, they overlook their own deficits of theory-of-mind.*

But perhaps I am just lacking empathy here.

A Two-Way Street? Theory-of-Mind

When people attribute thoughts and feelings to others, and display an appropriate emotional reaction,[3] we assume they empathise. Those who do not empathise in a customary manner are often viewed as indifferent. Empathising requires (to some degree) the skill known as 'mind reading', or theory-of-mind. This was at the heart of research into autism, because often autistic people are reported to struggle with understanding that other people do not think or feel the same as them (Frith, 2003). Put simply, having a well-developed 'theory-of-mind' suggests we attribute to people we meet thoughts and feelings other than our own: another person can know or feel things we do not; they may not know or feel what we know or feel. (The happy result of this means neurotypicals[4] can easily lie to people – this is both an evolutionary boon *and* a moral problem.) Evidence suggests some autistic children are delayed in developing 'theory-of-mind' or it is learned later. Brain imaging suggests reduced activation of some areas when autistic people face theory-of-mind tasks. This 'lack' of theory-of-mind is often referred to as 'mind-blindness'. (But we know there are degrees of visual ability, too.)

Many neurotypical children have a well-developed theory-of-mind (attributing thoughts and emotions to others becomes 'intuitive' early in their lives) that contributes to apparently 'seamless' social exchanges, whereas autistic children may have to work out the rules of social interactions logically. Increase the complexity of social interactions, however, and not 'intuitively' being skilled at 'mind-reading' is a fundamental challenge. (One way to think of this is that autistic children sometimes say what they see *regardless* of the feelings of others, whereas neurological children know the social benefits of

---

3   Of course the question here is who defines *appropriate* in a given situation. And if I don't respond how people think I should, will their view of me be 'he's just tired and so a little uninterested', or will they view me as pathologically 'odd' or 'indifferent' to their (often) quite dull self-obsessions, and so not answer my emails in the future. This is why I often will say, 'Oh, my goodness, that's terrible/great' (select as required) to people emoting, even if I have no idea who they are. Being empathic, like being altruistic, is beneficial (and so a little selfish) for the person being empathic and altruistic. And yet we accuse autistics for an apparent 'what's in it for me?' or 'who are you?' indifference. Go figure.

4   That is, people who are not autistic.

lying about how Grandfather smells[5] when he comes in from smoking his pipe in the back garden.)

Elizabeth Sheppard and colleagues questioned some of the rudimentary tropes still to be found concerning autism. They started from the existing evidence that autistic people respond differently from non-autistic people regarding social situations – autistic people have difficulties 'reading' the minds (or 'mental states' of others). But they wished to explore its opposite: how good are non-autistic people at 'reading' the minds of autistic people? It turns out not very good at all. Autistic people have equally expressive faces as neurotypicals, the study showed, but neurotypicals struggled to interpret the thinking of autistic people. The authors suggest autistic people experience a double-jeopardy: they start from a position of struggling to interpret the thinking of others who are struggling to interpret their thinking (Sheppard *et al.*, 2016). It turns out theory-of-mind is not fussy about where it finds it hard to find shelter.

And what I think of when I speak about autism, is 'And so?' because seamless social exchanges are perhaps not as common as we like to think, and intuitive is just another way to say 'learned then forgotten we learned'. So-called neurotypical seamless exchanges contain a degree of performance, a pinch of assumption, a sprinkling of recognising how we appear is perhaps more important that what we truly are. Autistic people may use more deductive approaches to working out others.

Uta Frith gives a telling example of the consequences of a not fully developed theory-of-mind:

> Josef took a trinket from a whole box of things by lucky dip and put it in a cup. He then ostentatiously let the child look inside, making it clear all the time that I (who sat at the other end of the table) was not allowed to look inside. He verified that this was understood by asking: 'Did you see what was in the cup?' and 'Did Uta see what was in the cup?' Now the critical questions were: 'Do you know what is in the cup?' and 'Does Uta know?' Astonishingly half of the autistic children who were tested, said, 'Yes, Uta knows [what is in the cup],' when I had not seen the object and could not have known. All were

---

5   That is, really bad. I mean utterly disgusting. But not to him. He smells of cherry wood to him.

at a mental age above that at which normal children could easily give the right answer. (Frith, 2003, p.213)

Note *half* of autistic children passed this simple test. This hypothetico-deductive method is more protracted than for a non-autistic child. Autistic people may be obliged to comprehend the benefits of ascribing to others independent thoughts and feelings *the slow way*. Make a social situation more complex and the 'processing lag' (or interpretation of what is expected) will take longer. For autistic people, understanding neurotypicals is hard and confounding work. Sometimes, it simply may not be worth the effort, and they stick to what they know.

Theory-of-mind is a description of an issue rather than an explanation (Bowler, 2007). Social interactions are more complex than simply saying someone passes through intuitive or hypothetico-deductive methods to arrive at the idea that others have their own knowledge or feelings. Some who see more fundamental issues impacting on people dispute theory-of-mind as an explanation of autism, but it *is* helpful in understanding what we might otherwise perceive as callous indifference in some humans. My own view, drawn from long personal experience, is this is far from a unique indicator of autism. Just watch the news.

(As presented throughout this book, human interactions are often communicative and a two-way street. Some communications are mutually beneficial – for example, interpreting a particular challenging behaviour as having a message – but this is not the case for all interactions. Neurotypicals are profoundly gifted at not telling the truth and manipulating others in order to accrue benefits. Neurotypicals seldom accuse themselves of pathological indifference to the welfare of others. (They simply accuse others.) Neurotypicals are skilled at 'morally disengaging' (or 'turning down' their own theory-of-mind) when encountering people in distress or people who need to do things that benefit the neurotypical. It is at best merely ironic that those considered normal – those who hold the power to label other humans as not normal – are often the cruellest of the neurotribes on our planet.)

If theory-of-mind holds as one of the central issues for an autistic person, imagine the potential impact on communication and social interactions: one might appear uninterested in the welfare of others, unwilling to communicate when from the perspective of the autistic person what the other person is saying is boring or not relevant. It can be argued then that theory-of-mind deficits are not unique to autistic people or other neurological conditions (we know people profoundly impacted by 'schizophrenia' likewise struggle with theory-of-mind tests) – but rather a matter of the significance of the impact. We've *all* got spiky profiles of skills to some degree, and we each struggle to understand others. We're all flawed. None of us can look in the mirror and proclaim ourselves perfect.

Neurotypicals communicate in a code called language that is often illogical but that they assume is *de rigueur*: the reality is neurotypicals often don't mean what they say or say what they mean. Neurotypicals survive by assuming contexts are as relevant to meaning as actual words: autistic people are often left bemused and alone in such exchanges (Wheelwright, 2007).

It could be the autistic child interprets literally what the neurologically typical child 'knows' alludes to something else when hearing the phrases, 'give me your hand' or 'let us toast the bride'. The autistic child may decode these startling words whereas a neurotypical child may 'know' what is intended.

What I think when I talk about autism is that I'm talking about humans, and whatever neurotribe a person is part of, there is 'a challenge of mutual understanding and a process of translation… Failure of understanding can go both ways. We have no idea what it is to see the world through the eyes of autism' (Happé, 2001, p.9). Vermeulen notes:

> resistance to changing our ideas about autism is sometimes greater than that seen in people with autism. So noted a young man with autism, too, and the way he formulates it is clear proof of two facts: (1) people with autism can have a driver's licence and (2) people with autism do have a sense of humour: 'In May of 1989 I drove 1,200 miles to attend the 10th annual TEACCH conference, where I learned that autistic people can't drive…' (Vermeulen, 2001, pp.24–25)

Gerland provides another example of how neurotypicals' own theory-of-mind abilities might be overstated:

if it looked like defiance, it had to be defiance. They measured me according to the way they measured themselves. They started with the premise that I was the same as they were, and if I wasn't really like them, then I ought to be. (Gerland, 1997, p.13)

Failing to understand one another is not a deficit owned by one neurotribe. Are neurotypicals so reliable that theirs is the only standpoint that counts? Do you think neurotypicals are *correct* to label autism a disability? Are neurotypicals so developmentally delayed they fail to understand the benefits of neurodiversity? This is what I think when I talk about autism: how come you work with autistic kids or adults and don't learn from them, that you remain unchanged when meeting other humans?

Identities are powerful forms of self-expression and being. Identities when imposed may become a defining (and perhaps limiting) characteristic justifying exclusion; when self-crafted, identities are a tool for liberation and inclusion.

So these are some of the things I think when I'm asked to talk about autism. I see fundamental differences in how the world is encountered because how we touch the universe and think about it is largely achieved through delicate neurology: our nervous systems join us to the physical world, the sensory world and the social world of ideas, memes, dogmas and experience. Tweak the neurology, tweak the lived experience: different neurologies are valid, I'd suggest.

None of us owns the truth or has the right to compare one spiky person against another, and claim one is normal, one is not. Why, doing so would be like my kids standing in the garden at night fighting over which of the flakes of snow they've caught is *the* most beautiful.

They know 'each one is beautiful', and they get the bigger picture, too, that arguing over flakes of snow distracts us from stopping in amazement at just how utterly remarkable it is to be alive, standing at night in a garden beneath falling snow. They also know in the morning each tiny flake of snow has contributed to a reshaping of the once familiar world.

We know snow is just bits of chemistry. And there's wonder in that. But there's also wonder in what flakes of snow falling from a dark sky taste, feel and look like, the ideas they trigger in our heads, the patterns they create when combining to carpet the garden. My children *all* know this, no matter who they are, no matter their gifts.

Possible Alternative or Competing Behaviours

Table 9.2: Possible Alternative or Competing Behaviours

Find functionally equivalent competing behaviours for...			
Behaviour	Function	Alternative 1	Alternative 2
Shouting	Gets attention	Hold up your hand	Press a button that makes a sound or lights up
Shouting	Escapes demands	Ask for a break	Shake your head
Hitting others	Gets a toy	Ask for toy	Go get toy yourself
Biting others	It feels good to bite	Chew a different item with equivalent properties	Ice or edible items
Picking and digging your own arm	It feels good to hurt myself – it makes me feel real	Elastic bands flicked on wrists	Hold ice in your hand for as long as you want
Sitting down in the road	Escapes shopping/gets a drink	Ask for a drink	Sit down on a bench next to the road

To be more effective than the challenging behaviour, remember the alternatives must be quicker and take less effort than the challenging behaviour and must have the same or closely similar outcome. Additionally, if the outcomes are socially mediated, people around the person must respond immediately to the alternative behaviour. Not doing so risks maintaining challenging behaviour.

References

Bennis, W.G. and Nanus, B. (1985) *Leaders: The Strategies for Taking Charge.* New York: Harper & Row.

Blaug, R. (2000) 'Blind hierarchism and radical organizational forms.' *New Political Science, 2,* 3, 379–396.

Blunden, R. (1988) 'Safeguarding quality.' In D. Towell (ed.) *An Ordinary Life in Practice: Developing Comprehensive Community-Based Services for People with Learning Disabilities.* London: King's Fund.

Bowler, D. (2007) *Autism Spectrum Disorders: Psychological Theory and Research.* Chichester: Wiley.

Bromley, J., Hare, D.J., Davison, K. and Emerson, E. (2004) 'Mothers supporting children with autistic spectrum disorders: social support, mental health status and satisfaction with service.' *Autism,* 8, 409–423.

Carr, E.G., Dunlap, G., Horner, R.H., Koegel, R.L., *et al.* (2002) 'Positive Behaviour Support: evolution of an applied science.' *Journal of Positive Behaviour Interventions,* 4, 1, 4–16.

Carr, E.G., Horner, R.H., Turnbull, A.P., Marquis, J.G., *et al.* (1999) *Positive Behaviour Support for People with Developmental Disabilities: A Research Synthesis.* Washington: AAMR.

Carr, E.G., Levin, L., McConnachie, G., Carlson, J.I., Kemp, D.C. and Smith, C.E. (1994) *Communication-Based Intervention for Problem Behaviour: A User's Guide for Producing Positive Change.* Baltimore: P.H. Brookes.

Clements, J. (2013) *Letters to the Home Front: Positive Thoughts and Ideas for Parents Bringing up Children with Developmental Disabilities, Particularly Those With an Autism Spectrum Disorder.* London: Jessica Kingsley Publishers.

Coupe, J. and Jolliffe, J. (1988) 'An early communication curriculum: implications for practice.' In J. Coupe and J. Goldbart (eds) *Communication Before Speech: Normal Development and Impaired Communication.* London: Croom Helm.

Covey, S.R. (2004) *The Seven Habits of Highly Effective People: Powerful Lessons in Personal Change.* London: Simon & Schuster.

Danforth, S. (2000) 'What can the field of developmental disabilities learn from Michel Foucault?' *Mental Retardation,* 38, 4, 364–328.

Delfos, M.F. (2005) *A Strange World – Autism, Asperger's Syndrome, and PDD-NOS: A Guide for Parents, Partners, Professional Carers, and People with ASDs.* London: Jessica Kingsley Publishers.

De Pry, R.L., Kamat, K.V. and Stock, R. (2015) 'Supporting individuals with challenging behaviour through systemic change.' In F. Brown, J.L. Anderson and R.L. De Pry (eds) *Individual Positive Behaviour Supports: A Standards-Based Guide to Practices in Schools and Community Settings.* Baltimore: Paul H. Brookes.

Deveau, R. and Leitch, S. (2018) *Person Centred Restraint Reduction: Developing Individual Restrictive Practice Reduction Plans: A Guide for Practice Leaders.* Birmingham: BILD.

Donnellan, A.M., LaVigna, G.W., Negri-Shoultz, N. and Fassbender, L. (1988) *Progress Without Punishment*. New York: Teachers College Press.

Egan, G. and Cowan, M.A. (1979) *People in Systems: A Model for Development in the Human-Services Professions and Education*. Belmont: Wadsworth.

Emerson, E. and Einfeld, S.L. (2011) *Challenging Behaviour*. Cambridge: CUP.

Emerson, E., Hatton, C., Bromley, J. and Caine, A. (1998) *Clinical Psychology and People with Intellectual Disabilities* (first edition). Chichester: Wiley.

Ephraim, G. (1998) 'Exotic communication, conversations, and scripts – or tales of the pained, the unheard and the unloved.' In D. Hewitt (ed.) *Challenging Behaviour: Principles and Practice*. London: David Fulton Publishers.

European Intellectual Disability Research Network (2003) *Intellectual Disability in Europe: Working Papers*. Canterbury: Tizard Centre, University of Kent.

Felce, D., Jones, E. and Lowe, K. (2002) 'Active support: planning daily activities and support for people with severe mental retardation.' In S. Holburn and P. Vietze (eds) *Person Centred Planning: Research, Practice and Future Directions*. Baltimore: Brookes.

Fleisher, L.S., Ballard-Krishnan, S.A. and Benito, N.F. (2015) 'Positive behaviour supports and quality of life.' In F. Brown, J.L. Anderson and R.L. De Pry (eds) *Individual Positive Behaviour Supports: A Standards-Based Guide to Practices in Schools and Community Settings*. Baltimore: Brookes.

Forrester-Jones, R., Cambridge, P., Carpenter, J., Tate, A., *et al.* (2006) 'The social networks of people with intellectual disability living in the community 12 years after resettlement from long-stay hospitals.' *Journal of Applied Research in Intellectual Disabilities*, 19, 4, 285–295.

Frith, U. (2003) *Autism: Explaining the Enigma* (second edition). Oxford: Blackwell.

Gerland, G. (1997) *A Real Person: Life on the Outside*. London: Souvenir Press.

Gilbert, T.F. (1978) *Human Competence: Engineering Worthy Performance*. New York: McGraw-Hill.

Grandin, T. (1995) *Thinking in Pictures: And Other Reports from My Life with Autism*. New York: Vintage Books.

Gray, K. and Sharratt, H. (2009) *Daisy: Eat Your Peas*. London: Red Fox Picture Books.

Green, S.E. (2007) 'We're tired, not sad: benefits and burdens of mothering a child with a disability.' *Social Science and Medicine*, 64, 150–163.

Halle, J.W. (1994) 'Foreword.' In E.G., Carr, R.H. Horner, A.P. Turnbull, J.G. Marquis, D.M. McLaughlin, M.L. McAtee, C.E. Smith, K.A. Ryan, M.B. Ruef, A. Doolabh and D. Braddock (1999) *Positive Behaviour Support for People with Developmental Disabilities: A Research Synthesis*. Washington: AAMR.

Happé, F. (2001) 'Foreword.' In P. Vermeulen, *Autistic Thinking: This is the Title*. London: Jessica Kingsley Publishers.

Hastings, R.P. and Taunt, H.M. (2002) 'Positive perceptions in families of children with developmental disabilities.' *American Journal on Mental Retardation*, 107, 116–127.

Hieneman, M. and Dunlap, G. (2015) in F. Brown, J.L. Anderson and R.L. De Pry (eds) *Individual Positive Behaviour Supports: A Standards-Based Guide to Practices in Schools and Community Settings*. Baltimore: Brookes.

Hingsburger, D. (1996) *Behaviour Self! Using Behavioural Concepts to Understand and Work with People with Developmental Disabilities*. Toronto: Diverse City Press.

Hingsburger, D. (1998) *Do? Be? Do? What to teach and how to teach people with developmental disabilities*. Toronto: Diverse City Press.

Holburn, S. and Vietze, P.M. (2002) 'A better life for Hal: five years of person centred planning and applied behaviour analysis.' In S. Holburn and P.Vietze (eds) *Person Centred Planning: Research, Practice and Future Directions*. Baltimore: Brookes.

Jackson, L. (2002) *Freaks, Geeks and Asperger's Syndrome: A User Guide to Adolescence*. London: Jessica Kingsley Publishers.

Jan, M and Girvin, J. (2002) 'The communication of neurological bad news to parents.' *Canadian Journal of Neurological Sciences*, 29, 78–82.

Johnston, T.C. (2014) *Behaviour Interventions Without Tears: Keeping FBAs and BIPs Simple.* Champaign: Research Press.

Kincaid, D. (1996) 'Person-centred planning.' In L.K. Koegel, R.L. Koegel and G. Dunlap (eds) *Positive Behavioural Support: Including People with Difficult Behaviour in the Community.* Baltimore: Paul H. Brookes Publishing Co.

Kincaid, D. (2017) PBS Is Not A Battle List of Strategies. Accessed July 2018, at www.youtube.com/watch?v=wAd-UWIqm7c.

Kincaid, D., Chapman, C., Shannon, P., Schall, C. and Harrower, J.K. (2002) 'Families and the Tri-State Consortium for Positive Behaviour Support.' In J.M. Lucyshyn, G. Dunlap and R.W. Albin (eds) *Families and Positive Behaviour Support: Addressing Problem Behaviour in Family Contexts.* Baltimore: Brookes.

Kincaid, D. and Fox, L. (2002) 'Person-centred planning and positive behaviour support.' In S. Holburn and P. Vietze (eds) *Person Centred Planning: Research, Practice and Future Directions.* Baltimore: Brookes.

LaVigna, G.W. (1995) *Emergency Management within a Non-Aversive Framework.* Los Angeles: IABA.

LaVigna, G.W. and Willis, T.J. (1997) 'Severe and challenging behaviour: counter-intuitive strategies for crisis management within a non-aversive framework.' *Positive Practices, 2,* 2.

LaVigna, G.W. and Willis, T.J. (2005) 'Multi-element model for breaking the barriers to social and community integration.' *Tizard Learning Disability Review,* 10, 2, 16–23.

Levinson, J. (2010) *Making Life Work: Freedom and Disability in a Community Group Home.* Minneapolis: UMP.

Li-Tsang, C.W-P., Yau, M. K-S. and Yuen, H.K. (2001) 'Success in parenting children with developmental disabilities: some characteristics, attitudes and adaptive coping skills.' *The British Journal of Developmental Disabilities,* 47, 2, 61–71.

Lovett, H. (1996) *Learning to Listen: Positive Approaches and People with Difficult Behaviour.* London: Jessica Kingsley Publishers.

MacDonald, A. and McGill, P. (2013) 'Outcomes of staff training in positive behaviour support: a systematic review.' *Journal of Developmental and Physical Disability,* 25, 17–33.

Mansell, J. and Beadle-Brown, J. (2012) *Active Support: Enabling and Empowering People with Intellectual Disabilities.* London: Jessica Kingsley Publishers.

Millar, S. and Aitkin, S. (2003) *Personal Communication Passports: Guidelines for Good Practice.* Edinburgh: University of Edinburgh. For further information, see www.communicationpassports.org.uk/Home.

Milton, D. (2012) 'On the ontological status of autism: the "double empathy problem".' *Disability and Society,* 27, 6, 883–887.

Mount, B. (1998) 'More than a meeting: benefits and limitations of personal futures planning.' In J. O'Brien and C. Lyle O'Brien (eds) *A Little Book About Person Centred Planning.* Toronto: Inclusion Press.

NHS (2018) Stopping Over Medication of People (with a learning disability, autism or both) (STOMP). Accessed July 2019, at www.england.nhs.uk/learning-disabilities/improving-health/stomp.

Nowlan, A. (2004) *Between Tears and Laughter: Selected Poems.* Hexham: Bloodaxe Books.

O'Brien, J. (1987) 'A guide to life-style planning: using the activities catalog to integrate services and natural support systems.' In B. Wilcox and G. Thomas Bellamy (eds) *A Comprehensive Guide to the Activities Catalog: An Alternative Curriculum for Youth and Adults with Severe Disabilities.* Baltimore: Brookes.

O'Brien, J. (2002) 'The ethics of person centred planning.' In S. Holburn, and P. Vietze (eds) *Person Centred Planning: Research, Practice and Future Directions.* Baltimore: Brookes.

O'Brien, J. and Lovett, H. (1992) *Finding A Way Toward Everyday Lives: The Contribution of Person Centered Planning.* Harrisburg, Pennsylvania: Pennsylvania Office of Mental Retardation.

O'Neill, R.E., Horner, R.H., Albin, R.W., Sprague, J.R., Storey, K. and Newton, J.S. (2015) *Functional Assessment and Program Development for Problem Behaviour: A Practical Handbook* (third edition). Pacific Grove, CA: Brooks/Cole.

Osgood, T. (2004) 'Doing It For Attention': Non Physical Reactive Strategies. Accessed July 2018, at http://tonyosgood.com/wp-content/uploads/2017/04/Doing-It-For-Attention.pdf.

Payne, R.A. (2000) *Relaxation Techniques: A Practice Handbook for the Health Care Professional* (second edition). London: Churchill Livingstone.

PBS Academy (2016) What Does Positive Behavioural Support Look Like? An Observational Checklist. Accessed July 20218, at http://pbsacademy.org.uk.

Pitonyak, D. (2005) Jumping into the Chaos of Things. Accessed July 2018, at www.dimagine.com/Jumping.pdf.

Pitonyak, D. (2007) Who Holds Your Story? Accessed July 2018, at http://dimagine.com/WhoHoldsYourStory.pdf.

Pitonyak, D. (2010a) 10 Things You Can Do To Support A Person With Difficult Behaviour. Accessed July 2018, at www.dimagine.com/10things.pdf.

Pitonyak, D. (2010b) The Importance of Belonging. Accessed July 2018, at www.dimagine.com/NASDDS.pdf. Also at www.dimagine.com/TASHbelonging.pdf.

Reid, D.H. and Green, C.W. (2006) 'Life Enjoyment, Happiness and Antecedent Behaviour Support.' In J.K. Luiselli (ed.) *Antecedent Assessment and Intervention: Supporting Children and Adults with Developmental Disabilities in Community Settings.* Baltimore: Brookes.

Risley, T. (1996) 'Get A Life! Positive behavioural intervention for challenging behaviour through life arrangement and life coaching.' in L.K. Koegel, R.L. Koegel and G. Dunlap (eds) *Positive Behavioural Support: Including People with Difficult Behaviour in the Community.* Baltimore: Brookes.

Sanderson, H., Kennedy, J., Ritchie, P. and Goodwin, G. (1997) *People, Plans and Possibilities.* Edinburgh: SHS.

Santelli, B., Ginsburg, C., Sullivan, S. and Niederhauser, C. (2002) 'A collaborative study of parent to parent programmes: implications for positive behaviour support.' In J.M. Lucyshyn, G. Dunlap and R.W. Albin (eds) *Families and Positive Behaviour Support: Addressing Problem Behaviour in Family Contexts.* Baltimore: Brookes.

Schulz, B. (2008) *The Street of Crocodiles and Other Stories.* London: Penguin.

Silberman, S. (2015) *Neurotribes: The Legacy of Autism and How to Think Smarter About People Who Think Differently.* Crows Nest: Allen & Unwin.

Singh, N.N., Lancioni, G.E., Winton, Adkins, A., Singh, J. and Singh, A. (2007) 'Mindfulness training assists individuals with moderate mental retardation to maintain their community placements.' *Behaviour Modification,* 31, 800–814.

Silverman, C. (2012) *Understanding Autism: Parents, Doctors and the History of a Disorder.* Princeton: PUP.

Shackleton, V. and Wale, P. (2000) 'Leadership and management.' In N. Chmiel (ed.) *Introduction to Work and Organisational Psychology: A European Perspective.* Oxford: Blackwell.

Sheppard, E., Pillai, D., Tze-Ling Wong, G., Ropar, D. and Mitchell, P. (2016) 'How easy is it to read the minds of people with autism spectrum disorder?' *Journal of Autism & Developmental Disorders,* 46, 1247–1254.

Summers, J.A., Behr, S.K. and Turnbull, A.P. (1989) 'Positive adaptations and coping strengths of families who have children with disabilities.' In G.H.S. Singer and L.K. Irvin (eds) *Support for Caregiving Families: Enabling Positive Adaptation to Disability.* Baltimore: Paul H. Brookes.

Sutton, R. (2010) *The No Asshole Rule: Building A Civilised Workplace and Surviving One that Isn't.* London: Piatkus.

Tincani, M. and Lorah, E.R. (2015) 'Defining, Measuring and Graphing Behaviour.' In F. Brown, J.L. Anderson and R.L. De Pry (eds) *Individual Positive Behaviour Supports: A Standards-Based Guide to Practices in Schools and Community Settings.* Baltimore: Paul H. Brookes.

Vanier, J. (2001) *Becoming Human.* Toronto: Anansi.

Vermeulen, P. (2001) *Autistic Thinking: This is the Title.* London: Jessica Kingsley Publishers.

Wagner, G.A. (2002) 'Person-centred planning from a behavioural perspective.' In S. Holburn and P. Vietze (eds) *Person Centred Planning: Research, Practice and Future Directions.* Baltimore: Brookes.

Wheelwright, S. (2007) 'Systemizing and empathising in autism spectrum conditions.' In J.M. Pérez, P.M. González, M.L. Comí and C. Nieto (eds) *New Developments in Autism: The Future is Today.* London: Jessica Kingsley Publishers.

Wing, L. (1998) 'The history of Asperger's syndrome.' In E. Schopler, G. Masibov and L.J. Kunce (eds) *Asperger's Syndrome or High Functioning Autism?* London: Plenum.

Worline, M.C. and Dutton, J.E. (2017) *Awakening Compassion at Work: The Quiet Power That Elevates People and Organisations.* Oakloand: Berrett-Koehler Publishers.

About the Author

Tony Osgood recently retired from work as Senior Lecturer in Intellectual and Developmental Disabilities at the University of Kent's Tizard Centre. From 2004 until 2019 he taught both undergraduate and postgraduate students on a range of topics including challenging behaviour, person-centred approaches and positive behaviour support. Before working in academia Tony was employed in an NHS psychology service, as well as in the private and voluntary sectors in both managerial and direct support roles. He now consults and writes full-time.

Tony has worked for thirty years in intellectual disabilities, autism, mental health and physical disability provision. He has written numerous accessible articles, taught across the UK, spoken at conferences and lectured internationally.

Tony is tall, bearded, married, and has four children; these are not, however, related.

For more information, visit http://tonyosgood.com.

Subject Index

Author Index